THE

Festive Christmas

COOKBOOK

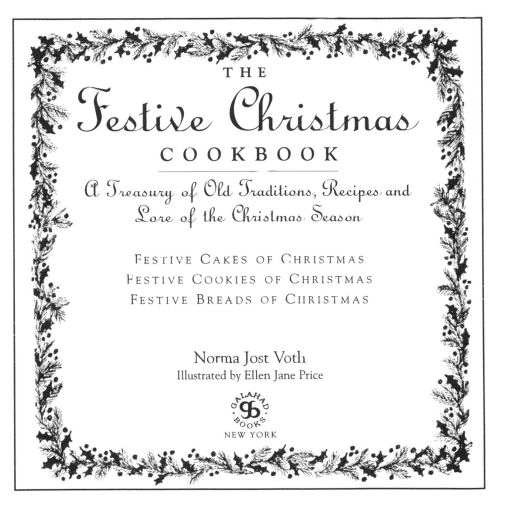

THE
Festive Christmas
COOKBOOK

A Treasury of Old Traditions, Recipes and
Lore of the Christmas Season

FESTIVE CAKES OF CHRISTMAS
FESTIVE COOKIES OF CHRISTMAS
FESTIVE BREADS OF CHRISTMAS

Norma Jost Voth
Illustrated by Ellen Jane Price

GALAHAD
BOOKS
NEW YORK

First Galahad Books edition published in 1996.

Galahad Books
A division of BBS Publishing Corporation
386 Park Avenue South
New York, NY 10016

Galahad Books is a registered trademark of BBS Publishing Corporation.

Published by arrangement with Herald Press, Scottdale, PA 15683.

Library of Congress Catalog Card Number: 96-78200

ISBN: 0-88365-973-5

Printed in the United States of America.

Contents

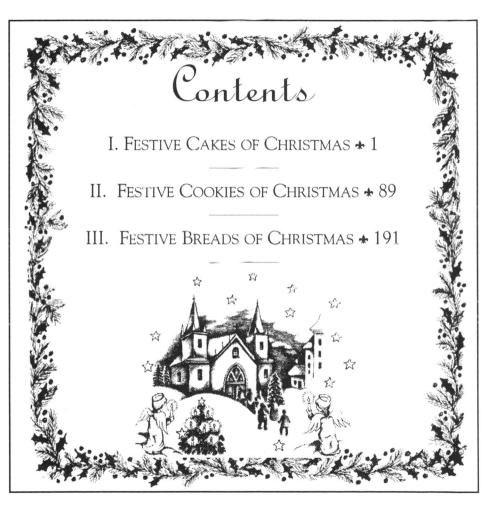

FESTIVE Cakes of CHRISTMAS

Dear Reader,

As you browse through this book, may you, too, come to appreciate the beauty of Christmases past.

Without exception, the women who shared memories of Christmases in other lands, spoke with a nostalgia, a fondness, almost a reverence as they recalled the traditions, the baking, the family rituals handed down to them through many generations.

Whatever your heritage—learn about it. Talk with your grandparents, great uncles and aunts, about their early Christmas traditions—especially if they lived in another country. From them you will gain a better understanding of your family and the heritage which is yours.

And if possible, pass on to your children in some tangible way the beauty, security, and warmth that come from preserving those Christmas traditions of the past.

Norma Jost Voth
San Jose, California

To my husband, Alden, who willingly tastes, tests, and critiques Christmas baking all year long—with gratitude for support and encouragement.

ACKNOWLEDGMENTS: Special thanks to Adaline Karber, caterer, and Anne Hyrne for their expertise and enthusiasm in testing recipes; to Sara Fisher (Amish), Catherine Weidner (Moravians), Eldress Bertha Lindsay (Shakers), Joyce Marsh (England), Esther Harvest and Johanna Reynolds (Denmark), Terttu Gilbert (Finland), Anne Marie Boube, Marthe Nussbaumer, and Esther Dickler (France), Magdalena Meyer and Doris Walter (Germany), Aristea Pettis (Greece), Eithne Cuckel and Marie Martinez (Ireland), Rosa Cavillo (Mexico), and Marie Halun Bloch (Ukraine), for their helpful contributions.

In earlier times the season of Christmas was long, stretching from St. Thomas' Day—when cooks begin in earnest to prepare their plum puddings—to the blessing of the candles on Candlemas. In Scandinavia, the Danes still celebrate "the month of Christmas."

Indeed, it is more than a hurried day or two. Christmas is a season, a holy festival to be celebrated and savored, to be held long enough to feel the deep, moving significance of this holy time.

And who can keep such a time of festivity without good food? The feeling that good food is necessary to make a good festival has long been with us. Carols sing of it, ballads list delicacies to be eaten for the celebration. Probably more tasty foods and lovely pastries are prepared for the feast of Christmas than any other.

In these pages is a collection of hallowed traditions, anecdotes, and fanciful cakes and tarts typical of the season, gathered from many countries. May they add richness to your own family's cherished traditions.

The Christmas Season

From Advent to Candlemas

Advent

Advent begins with the fourth Sunday before Christmas. These four weeks are a time of spiritual preparation, heralding the coming of Christ into the world.

"*Prepare the way of the Lord*" (Matthew 3:3).

European children eagerly count the long days before Christmas by opening tiny numbered doors on Advent calendars. Inside are secret pictures, little messages, or even small presents.

Advent wreaths, fashioned of evergreens and decorated with four candles, hang in living rooms and adorn dining tables throughout Northern Europe. Each Advent Sunday a candle is lighted—until all are burning—making it a lovely time for family and friends to gather around the wreath to sing the old Advent songs and sample the first Christmas cookies.

For European homemakers, Advent is a busy season of cleaning, baking, and preparing for the holiday. German women, especially, take great pains with their *Weihnachts Gebäck* (Christmas baking).

Everywhere these four weeks before Christmas are looked upon as a preparation for the greatest festival of the Christian year.

St. Nicholas' Day

December 6, St. Nicholas' Day for European children is the time for presents. In Holland, Sint Nikolaas, as he is called there, arrives in harbor cities by boat and is greeted by the mayor and cheered by thousands of children and adults. He rides into the city on horseback, dressed in a white robe and bishop's golden mitre. With him are *swarte pieten* (servants) wearing puffed breeches and plumed hats. One carries a bag of presents, peppernuts, cookies, and a birch rod. In Amsterdam they lead a parade to the royal palace.

On St. Nikolaas Eve Dutch children put out hay and carrots for the good saint's horse and neatly set their shoes before the fireplace, hoping for gifts. But, if Katy has been lazy or young Diedrich impolite, St. Nikolaas knows all—and *Swarte Piet* (Black Peter) leaves a birch switch instead of sweets.

Fact and legend mix, but there actually was a generous Bishop Nikolaos, born in Patara, Turkey, more than 1,700 years ago. He left a wealthy home to serve the church and was known as a loving, compassionate man who helped the poor. It is said he remembered needy children with gifts on their doorsteps at night, without them knowing where the presents came from.

Europe celebrates his day and remembers his kind deeds by giving gifts.

To Christmas festivities, Americans have added a yearly visit from Santa Claus. It was Dutch settlers who brought the custom of celebrating the Feast of St. Nicholas to this country. But St. Nicholas of Holland gradually changed from the thin, stately, robed man to the jolly Santa our children know. Three men contributed to this change: Washington Irving (1809) pictured Santa as a chubby fellow riding through the air in a sleigh drawn by reindeer; Dr. Clement Moore (1822) composed the "Visit from St. Nicholas" for his children. In 1865 Thomas Nash illustrated Moore's poem in *Harper's Weekly* and gave us the white bearded, jolly old Santa in his red, fur-trimmed coat.

St. Lucia's Day

December 13, St. Lucia's Day, is celebrated in Scandinavia, and especially Sweden, as "The Feast of Light." Every Swedish home has a lovely early morning Lucia ceremony.

Up before dawn, the eldest daughter of the family is Lucia for the day. She dons a flowing white gown and wears a crown of lingenberry leaves with white candles on her head. Carrying a tray of steaming coffee and fragrant golden saffron buns and *pepparkakor,* Lucia goes from room to room singing Lucia songs and wakening the family with breakfast in bed.

Every school, village, and city has its Lucia Queen who presides over parades or day-long festivities.

Lucia's legend came to Sweden from Italy and honors a fourth-century girl who died a Christian martyr after distributing her dowry to the poor on the eve of her wedding. In Italy, Lucia is remembered with bonfires and torchlight parades.

Christmas Eve

December 24 is Christmas Eve or Holy Evening. In many countries shops and stores close by midafternoon. Streets are deserted and silent while families gather at home to celebrate the humble birth of Christ in a stable in Bethlehem.

Every country has its Christmas Eve rituals, but none more than Poland. At dusk, children watch anxiously for the first star to appear. Only then may the Christmas Eve supper with its twelve symbolic dishes begin. Before eating, Polish fathers share *oplateks*, rice wafers blessed by the priest. Each family member, from oldest to youngest, is greeted with a special Christmas wish.

In Ireland, tall candles glow from every window on Christmas Eve, lighting the traveler to Bethlehem.

Townspeople and choirs in the tiny Alpine village of Oberndorf, Austria, celebrate the anniversary of "Silent Night" outside the chapel where Franz Gruber played the organ (1818).

All over the world, worshipers gather at midnight church services to hear again the familiar Christmas story and sing carols of Jesus' birth.

December 24–25 was declared officially to be the birth of Christ by proclamation of Pope Julius I, in the year 350. It coincided with the time of the winter solstice, the season of the Roman Saturnalia.

Christmas Day, December 25

And Joseph ... went up from Galilee, from the city of Nazareth, to Judea, to the city of David, which is called Bethlehem ... to be enrolled with Mary, his betrothed, who was with child. And while they were there, the time came for her to be delivered. And she gave birth to her first-born son and wrapped him in swaddling cloths, and laid him in a manger, because there was no place for them in the inn. Luke 2:4-7.

Boxing Day

December 26, Boxing Day in England, comes from the old custom of putting money in small boxes for servants, the postman, milkman, and the like.

A century ago, when English village streets were very narrow, it was customary for tradespeople to walk though the streets with their boxes attached to long poles, making it convenient for people to drop gifts of money.

Traditionally, these gift boxes were made of metal, cardboard, or papier-mâché in shapes of squares or hexagons, and were distinguished by a generous, inviting slit. Antique boxes may still be found in British museums.

Today businesses close on Boxing Day, providing a time for the British to watch rugby, to see a pantomime (usually a children's fairy tale) in a London theater, to visit relatives, entertain, or go fox hunting in the country.

St. Stephen's Day

December 26, St. Stephen's Day in Ireland, honors Stephen, the first Christian martyr. Earlier it was known as "Wrenning Day," a time when they stoned a wren in commemoration of this saint. In some counties, children go about in costume, asking for "help to bury the wren."

This also is a day for children's pantomimes in large downtown theaters.

In other European countries, December 26 is the Second Day of Christmas, a time to begin a round of visits to friends and relatives. Christmas trees are not brought into the home until December 24, so the rest of the week is given to parties and family gatherings. Little work is done. "Christmas seems to hold on a little longer there," says Marie Martinez, of her childhood in Ireland.

New Year's Eve and Day

December 31 & January 1. On New Year's Eve and Day churches may hold "watch night services," with hymns, prayers, and communion.

For most people, this is a time of new resolutions, with lists of ways to make the coming year better. At midnight bells toll, fireworks may light the sky, and people go about wishing each other a happy new year.

In Holland, Dutch women stir up batches of Olliebollen—fat golden raisin fritters—to serve with pots of hot coffee on New Year's Day.

THE FEAST OF ST. BASIL is celebrated in Greek Orthodox churches on New Year's Day. Presents are given on this day, rather than on Christmas. Basil, one of the great fathers of the Catholic and Orthodox churches, is remembered for founding orphanages, hospitals, and schools. A handsome cake, *Vasilopita* (St. Basil's cake, p.76), is brought to the church and blessed in a vesper ceremony. At the stroke of midnight (New Year's Eve) the *Vasilopita*, baked with a hidden fortune coin inside, is served according to old ritual.

16

The Feast of Epiphany

January 6, The Feast of Epiphany or *Little Christmas*, is a holy festival honoring the wise men coming to the infant Jesus.

> And lo, the star, which they saw in the east, went
> before them, till it came and stood over where
> the young child was. When they saw the star,
> they rejoiced with exceeding great joy.
> Matt. 2:9b–11.

This day is also known as *Three Kings' Day, Feast of the Magi,* and *Twelfth Night,* the traditional English Name—the twelfth night after Christmas.

For many Eastern rite churches, this day commemorates the baptism of Jesus in a special service. If there is a nearby body of water, the priest may lead a procession to a lake or river for the "Blessing of the Water." Some Eastern churches still celebrate Epiphany according to the old Julian calendar, which falls on our January 18.

Polish people write the letters KMB above their doorways to remind all who enter of the coming of the wise men.

In Italy, Epiphany is called *Old Christmas* and gifts are exchanged. Children hang their stockings and wait for the good witch, *Le Befana,* to bring their toys.

Epiphany usually marks the close of the twelve days of Christmas.

17

St. Knut's Day

January 13, St. Knut's Day in Scandinavia, ends the Yule season and a month of Christmas. In Sweden the tree is dismantled and children may choose a prize of cookies or candy from the decorations. Carols are sung and there is a last dance around the tree. With singing and much laughter, the tree is taken out the door with the wish:

> May God bless your Christmas.
> May it last till Easter.

Candlemas Day

February 2, Candlemas Day. Many years ago the Feast of Purification of the Virgin (a ritual required by Jewish law 40 days after the birth of a child) was chosen by the Pope as a day for the blessing of candles people carried in processions before mass. The day is observed in Greek, Roman Catholic, and Protestant Episcopal churches.

In Mexico, the person who finds a large bean or china doll in his slice of Three Kings' Cake (January 6) must host a party on Candlemas.

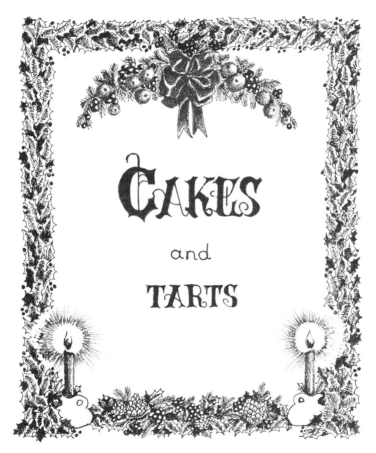

CAKES

and

TARTS

A special kind of excitement filled Mother's kitchen in late November—there was a new feeling of warmth, a kind of spicy expectancy of good things to come.

Evenings when a cold, blustery wind howled outside were perfect for sorting through the recipe box and thumbing through the old, hand-written cookbook with its pages of fruit cake and honey cookies recipes.

There were cozy times of sitting at the oak table helping chop fruit and raisins, cracking and shelling nuts, and crushing fresh spices in the grinder. Some evenings there were bowls brimming with fruit to be mixed with a fragrant batter, crocks to be packed with dough to age and mellow before baking.

Best of all were the times when the first baking came from the oven and we welcomed cookies slightly burned or shaved off tiny slivers of fruit cake. Later there would be evenings with chairs pulled up to the kitchen table to celebrate the Christmas baking with a fresh table cloth, a lighted candle, and a steaming pot of coffee.

Indeed, Christmas baking was special, for those were delicacies to be baked and eaten only once a year.

Yule Cake

Lavishly studded with colorful fruits and whole nuts, this recipe, from a former neighbor, Thelma Luckenbill, Upland, California, is a family favorite.

1½ cups Brazil nuts, whole	½ cup candied green cherries
1½ cups walnut halves	½ cup seedless raisins
1 cup pitted dates	¾ cup flour
1 cup candied orange peel, chopped	¾ cup sugar
½ cup candied red cherries	½ tsp. baking powder
	½ tsp. salt
	3 eggs
	1 tsp. vanilla

Grease 9×5×3-inch loaf pan; line bottom with parchment. Place fruit and nuts in large bowl. Sift dry ingredients over fruit and mix well. Beat eggs until light; add vanilla. Blend into fruit mixture. Spoon into loaf pan; spread evenly. Bake at 300° for 2 hours or until firm. Brush with Karo syrup to glaze. Cool 10 minutes in pan. Remove and cool on rack. Store in foil to age.

Lil's Light Fruit Cake

Lillian Proceviat has a wide repertoire of Ukrainian / American Christmas baking specialties, but this is her family's favorite cake. "My children don't care for citron, so I make this cake for them."

1 cup sweet butter	2½ cups flour
1 cup sugar	½ cup red maraschino cherries, diced
5 eggs	½ cup green maraschino cherries, diced
¼ tsp. mace	½ cup pecans, coarsely chopped
1 tsp. vanilla or ½ tsp. almond extract	

Bring butter and eggs to room temperature. Sift flour and measure. Drain, chop, and dry cherries on paper towels. In one cup of the flour, dredge cherries and pecans; shake off excess flour and retain for cake. Cream butter and sugar until light and fluffy. Add eggs, one at a time, beating hard after each addition. Add spice and flavoring. (Mrs. Proceviat also suggests ¼ cup rum or brandy as an alternate.) Mix well.

Add flour, a small amount at a time, using flour from fruit and nuts. Beat hard until batter is smooth. Gently fold in fruit and nuts, spreading colors of cherries evenly. Spoon batter into greased and floured loaf pan. Bake at 275° for 1½ hours or until done. Cool on rack. Brush with glaze. Decorate with candied cherries and whole pecans. Store in foil.

—*Mrs. Proceviat is the owner of The Kiev Kitchen, Mountain View, California.*

New England Cranberry Tarts

3 cups cranberries	1 tbsp. orange rind, grated
½ cup raisins	1 cup water
1½ cups sugar	Topping
2 tbsp. cornstarch	Pastry 2 crust, 9-inch pie

Prepare pie crust pastry and chill. Cut 10–12 circles with 4½ inch cutter. Press circles into tart or 2½-inch muffin pans. In saucepan combine cranberries, raisins, orange rind and water. Simmer 3 minutes. Mix together sugar and cornstarch; stir into cranberries. Cook and stir until thick and bubbly. Spoon into tart shells. Combine ¾ cup flour, ⅓ cup sugar; cut in 6 tbsp. butter until crumbly. Sprinkle over tarts. Bake at 400° for about 15–20 minutes or until golden brown.

Hal Bohannon's Chocolate Spice Cake

A luscious chocolate chiffon cake, topped with whipped cream, makes an elegant addition to a New Year's buffet. The recipe comes from the menu of the old Bohannon Restaurant, well know in San Jose, California. After retiring, Mr. Bohannon taught cooking classes in this area, sharing his secrets, recipes, and skills from a lifetime of good cooking.

½ cup sweet chocolate, ground	1 tsp. cinnamon
¾ cup boiling water	7 eggs, separated
1½ cups flour	½ cup salad oil
1¾ cups sugar	2 tsp. orange peel, grated
4 tsp. baking powder	½ tsp. cream of tartar
¾ tsp. salt	1 cup walnuts, finely chopped
2 tsp. allspice	Whipping cream

Stir chocolate and boiling water until dissolved and smooth. Cool. Sift together flour, 1½ cups sugar, baking powder, salt, allspice, and cinnamon. Make a well in the dry ingredients and add egg yolks, oil, orange peel, and chocolate mix. Stir until smooth. Beat egg whites until foamy, add cream of tartar, and gradually beat in remaining sugar. Beat to stiff peak stage and gently fold into the chocolate mixture. Sprinkle nuts on top and fold in. Bake in an ungreased 10-inch tube pan at 350° for about 1 hour. Invert pan and cool. Frost with chocolate buttercream or whipped cream.

To decorate with whipped cream, cut a well or "trench" 1 inch wide and 1 inch deep in the top of the cake. Scoop out pieces of cake from well. Fill with whipped cream. Fill pastry bag with remaining cream and using Open Star Pastry Tube #1 make swirls over the filled well and around the base of the cake with whipped cream. Top the swirls with 8-10 drained long-stemmed red maraschino cherries.

Old Order Amish Christmas Dinner for 80

Roast Turkey with Fried Bread Dressing
Giblet Gravy
Mashed Potatoes   Fried Sweet Potatoes
Buttered Noodles
Lima Beans   Peas
Dried Corn in Cream   Mixed Vegetables
Seven Day Sweet Pickles
Banana Pickles   Chow Chow   Spiced Cantaloupe
Homemade Bread
Apple Sauce   Fruit Salad
Cornstarch Pudding
Angel Cake with Butter Cream Frosting
Date Cake   Carrot Cake
Lemon Sponge Pie   Mince Pie
Cherry Pie   Blueberry Pie
Coffee   Chocolate Covered Pretzels

"In our family it is common to have 80 guests or more for Christmas dinner," says Sara Fisher, who grew up in an Old Order Amish home. "Married family, children, aunts, uncles, grandparents, all are invited. But then, our homes are built to accommodate 200 people for church services, so we are set up for big groups.

"Long before Christmas the ladies get together to plan the menu and what to bring. Guests always 'sit up to tables' and dinner is served in sittings—the older men first, then younger men and boys. Little boys under six sit with their fathers. Young mothers and girls serve, and the table is set and respread in a short time.

"When the dishes are done, we gather in the living room to sing the old German Christmas hymns until it is time to go home. Before leaving, there is a snack of cookies and coffee."

Amish women are known for their good Pennsylvania-Dutch style cooking; the men are industrious, thrifty farmers. The Amish teach separation from the world, personal simplicity. Some groups farm with horses and live without electricity, telephones, and autos.

—*Sara Fisher is a teacher in an Old Order Amish school near Soudersburg, Pennsylvania*

Amish Date-Nut Cake

Popular among Amish families in the Lancaster area of Pennsylvania, this cake, served with whipped cream, makes a nice substitute for traditional fruit cake.

1 pound walnut meats, coarsely chopped	2 tsp. baking powder
1 pound dates, chopped	1 cup sugar
1 cup flour	4 eggs, separated
½ tsp. salt	1 tsp. vanilla
	Glaze

Place dates and nuts in large bowl; sift dry ingredients over fruit and nuts. Blend well. Stir in well-beaten egg yolks and vanilla. Beat egg whites until stiff peaks form. Fold into batter. Pour into greased 9×5×3-inch loaf pan. Bake at 350° for about 1½ hours or until done. Brush with Karo syrup while hot. Decorate with candied cherries and blanched almonds. Cool in pan 10 minutes. Serve with whipped cream.

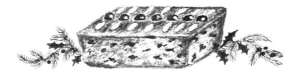

Moravian Christmas

In Moravian Communities it is the tradition to go *putzing* during the Christmas season. Homes are open to visitors, so families drop in on their friends to admire each other's Christmas *putz* (crèche).

For many years the Moravians have used these manger scenes as a beautiful way of telling the Christmas story to children, their neighbors, and friends. Sometimes a whole room is given over to the *putz*, which is often built on a raised platform. Moss, rocks, old tree stumps, and evergreens form a background for beautiful hand-carved wooden figures from Germany. Whenever visitors come in, a member of the family reads the Christmas story.

The word *putz*, which means "to decorate," comes from a German dialect.

Moravians in the Christmas city of Bethlehem, Pennsylvania, also decorate a large community *putz* at the Central Moravian Church, attracting thousands of visitors each December. Neighborhoods all over that city glow with single lighted candles in windows of Moravian (and other) homes from the first Sunday of Advent throughout the Christmas season.

Moravian Sugar Cake (p. 30) is served at home and at church meetings during the holidays and all through the year.

Catherine Weidner's Moravian Sugar Cake

Originally made by the early settlers, Moravian Sugar Cake is served at weddings, social affairs, and holidays in the Bethlehem, Pennsylvania, area. Catherine Weidner, who is married to Pastor Mervin Weidner of Central Moravian Church in Bethlehem, shares her family recipe.

1 pkg. active dry yeast	½ tsp. salt
1 cup warm potato water	6-7 cups flour
1 cup sugar	1 lb. light brown
½ cup shortening	sugar
½ cup butter or margarine	½ cup butter
3 eggs, beaten	Cinnamon, nutmeg
1 cup warm mashed potatoes	Evaporated milk

Pare, slice, and boil 2 or 3 potatoes. Drain (saving water) and mash. Cool to lukewarm. Sprinkle yeast in 1 cup potato water; dissolve. Cream shortening, butter, and sugar until fluffy. Add eggs and mix well. Add potatoes, salt, yeast and warm potato water and mix. Gradually add about 3-3½ cups flour and beat 5 minutes with electric mixer. Gradually add 3 more cups flour. Turn out on floured board and knead until smooth and elastic, about 8-10 minutes. Place dough in greased bowl, turning to grease top. Cover with kitchen towel and set in warm place until double in bulk (about 1½-2 hours). Punch down and knead lightly.

Divide dough into 4 pieces and pat into 4 greased 9×9-inch pans (or 2 large rectangular pans). Cover and let rise in warm place until light and puffy, but not quite double. With thumb, make indentations in cakes and push small pieces of butter into holes. Cover entire top with light brown sugar; then sprinkle with cinnamon and a bit of nutmeg. Repeat on each cake. Dot with more butter. Drizzle lightly with evaporated milk or cream. Bake at 350° for about 20 minutes or until golden brown. Cool. Serve warm.

The Moravian Christmas Putz

31

𝔖𝔥𝔞𝔨𝔢𝔯 ℭ𝔥𝔯𝔦𝔰𝔱𝔪𝔞𝔰

Early Shakers celebrated Christmas as a time of giving and for-giving. Not only was their communal dwelling to be polished and scrubbed for this holy day, but the sisters and brothers were to "sweep the house of the spirit," and "wash from the floor the stains of sin," sometimes using imaginary mops and brooms. All members were to make reconciliation, leave grudges behind, remember the poor, and keep the day sacred. For the children, there were imaginary gifts often accompanied by pantomime—"cakes of love," "gold of golden plums," and "clusters of grapes filled with the love of God."

—From the Shaker Order of Christmas.

Sister Lucy Ann's Christmas Cake

Sister Lucy Ann Shepard's spice cake is included in a little book of *Shaker Tested Recipes* from the Canterbury Village in New Hampshire. Eldress Bertha Lindsay fondly remembers Lucy Ann "as a beautiful sister, involved in the ministry, and a trustee of our group." She must have enjoyed a turn in the kitchen as well, making Christmas cake.

1 cup butter	1 tsp. cinnamon
1 cup sugar	1 cup candied fruits or
6 eggs	citron, chopped
1¾ cups flour	1 cup currants
1½ tsp. baking powder	½ cup orange juice or
1 tsp. allspice	apple juice

Cream butter and sugar until light and fluffy. Add eggs, one at a time, beating well. Sift dry ingredients together and add to batter. Drain fruits and dredge in flour; shake off excess. Add fruits and orange juice to batter; mix thoroughly. Pour into well-greased and floured tube pan. Bake at 350° for 1 hour or until done.

Cool. Store in foil. Before serving, glaze with powdered sugar and lemon juice. Decorate with candied cherries. (Sister Lucy Ann used brandy in place of orange juice in her cake.)

Christmas at Canterbury Village

Shaker Eldress, Bertha Lindsay, remembers Christmases at the Canterbury Village (New Hampshire) when the choir came into the dining room singing carols Christmas morning. "We started in the attic, and made our way down to the dining room in two groups, singing all the way, meeting at our tables.

"The sisters used to have their little rooms festooned with red and green and white, and the children's workshop was always festive with greenery and presents. One year we had a peach tree with stuffed birds. We made simple gifts for our teachers and sisters.

"Each year I wrote a letter to the sister who took care of me. Bible stories were dramatized in the chapel on Christmas Eve, and Christmas Day, after a lovely dinner of turkey and 'all the fixings,' we just enjoyed our presents."

Dedicated to hard work, thrift, and celibacy, Shakers wore plain clothes and led quiet lives in communal villages. They made outstanding contributions to simple furniture design and agricultural advancement. "Give your hands to work and your hearts to God" was a creed they lived.

Eldress Lindsay came to the Shaker village at the age of eight, when her mother died. Now 83, she is one of the nine elderly sisters who remain from this once thriving group.

In our little country school in Kansas we always had a Christmas program, Helen Epp of Newton, Kansas, reminisces. It was thrilling to have a tree with real candles and watch the older men guard it with wet cotton on long sticks. We gladly took the job of stringing popcorn and cranberries for the tree—an excuse not to do our schoolwork.

Everyone had dialogues and poems (called a *Wünsch*), to recite—sometimes more than one. The longer, the better. The more you could say, the smarter you were!

After the program there were sacks with treats. "An orange was really something precious. I always kept mine until it was about dried out—until my brother George would get so hungry for it he couldn't stand it anymore. Then I sold it to him and he gave me money for it!"

Silent night, Holy night

Austria's Gift to the World

A broken church organ prompted the composing of the world's most popular Christmas carol, "Silent Night." It was December 23, 1818, when Pastor Josef Mohr discovered mice had chewed holes in the bellows of the church organ. To have some music for the Christmas Eve mass, Mohr quickly wrote the words for a simple song and showed them to his good schoolmaster friend, Franz Gruber. A few hours later, Gruber had set the words to music for two voices, choir, and guitar—a "worldly" instrument never used in church before.

For the first time on December 25, the two men sang "Silent Night," accompanied only by Gruber's guitar and a small choir.

Every Christmas Eve at 5:00 p.m., the Choral Society of Oberndorf (near Salzburg in the Austrian Tyrol) sings a memorial concert around a lighted Christmas tree outside the tiny memorial chapel where this hymn was written.

Viennese Sachertorte

Served in the coffee room of the Sacher Hotel, Vienna, this simple but elegant cake was invented in 1832 by master sugar baker, Franz Sacher. A chocolate-lover's delight, *Sachertorte* (Zahk-er-tohr-teh) is a chocolate-rich sponge cake, filled or coated with apricot jam and glazed with dark, bittersweet chocolate. Viennese add a side serving of *Schlagobers*, or whipped cream.

6 oz. semi-sweet chocolate	8 egg yolks
1 cup sweet butter	1 cup flour
1 cup confectioners' sugar	10 egg whites
½ tsp. vanilla	1 cup apricot jam
	Chocolate glaze
	Whipping cream

Preheat oven to 325°. Butter two 9-inch round cake pans and line with circles of wax paper; butter and sprinkle paper with flour. Shake off excess flour. Chop chocolate into small pieces. Melt over double boiler. Cream butter; blend in sugar and vanilla. Blend in chocolate. Add egg yolks, 1 at a time, beating well after each addition. Gradually add sifted flour to chocolate mixture. With egg whites at room temperature, beat until stiff peaks form (not dry). Mix about ⅓ of egg whites into the chocolate mixture, then pour the chocolate over the remaining egg whites. Fold in with rubber spatula, using a cutting motion until no trace of white remains. Do not overfold. Pour batter into cake pans and bake 25-30 minutes at 325° or until cake is done. Remove from pans and cool.

Heat apricot jam to boiling. Strain through a fine strainer or place in blender. Place lower layer of cake on rack over a baking sheet. Spread with apricot jam. Place second layer on top. Spread top and sides with jam.

Glaze: 3 oz. unsweetened chocolate, 1 cup whipping cream, 1 cup sugar, 1 tsp. corn syrup, 1 egg, 1½ tsp. vanilla extract. Break chocolate into small pieces. In heavy saucepan combine broken pieces of chocolate, cream, sugar, and corn syrup. Cook over low heat, stirring constantly until sugar melts. Increase heat to medium and cook without stirring until a few drops of mixture form a soft ball in cold water. Beat egg lightly and stir in small amounts of chocolate, stirring rapidly. Return chocolate to saucepan and stir briskly. Cook over low heat until mixture coats wooden spoon. Add vanilla. Pour over cake, evenly coating sides. Refrigerate 3-4 hours. Remove 1 hour before serving. Offer with side serving of whipped cream.

Treasures from the Tyrol

In writing of family Christmases in their Alpine home in Austria, the Baroness Maria Von Trapp recalls a large crib placed in the living room during Advent. At first it would be empty, she says, but always there was a big bagful of straw beside it. Every evening, after prayers, each child took as many pieces of straw as he had done good deeds during the day and added them to the crib.

"When it was finally standing under the Christmas tree cradling the 'Baby wrapped in swaddling clothes,' the Holy Child seemed to smile at the children, grateful for the soft, warm bed prepared with so much love.... You may be very grown up, and even white-haired, but all during Advent you will feel the same urge to 'collect more straws for the crib'" (from "Christmas with the Trapp Family").

In many places in the snow-covered Tyrol, the darkness of Christmas Eve is brightened by hundreds of torches as village families make their way down the mountain to their little churches. The nighttime stillness is broken only by the crunching of boots across the snow, soft whispers, and the joyous songs of carolers, singing from church towers and the village square.

After mass, a warm fire, a festive supper, and their beloved *Weihnachtsbaum* (Christmas tree) welcome families at home.

The Month of Christmas

One of the things that stands out in my memory of childhood Christmases in Denmark is that things were done leisurely and over a long period of time. For *The Month of Christmas*, as December is still called in Denmark, my mother prepared a special "work calendar." One particular Christmasy task was allotted to each day.

Make Christmas cards
Make tree ornaments
Go on snow picnic to collect
  green branches
Wrap parcels for post

Wrap parcels for family
Bake pebernødder
Go to town to see
  Christmas lights
Make baskets for cookie
  presents for neighbors

What has lasted in my memory, and what I have tried to pass on to my own children, is this sense of joyous expectation without too much hectic rush and bustle, this sense of savoring *The Month of Christmas* leisurely so that no one is worn out when the time comes to celebrate the birth of Christ.—*Johanna Reynolds.*

Danish Almond Cake

Among the traditional Christmas desserts in Denmark is this tasty almond cake topped with chocolate glaze. Esther Harvest, Los Gatos, California, brought the recipe from her mother's home in Copenhagen.

1 cup butter or margarine	⅛ tsp. salt
1 cup sugar	1 tsp. baking powder
2 eggs	3 tsp. almond extract
1¼ cups flour	⅓ cup boiling water
	Chocolate glaze

Cream butter and sugar until fluffy. Add eggs and mix well. Gradually add flour sifted with baking powder and salt. Beat thoroughly. Add almond extract and boiling water. Mix well. Pour into greased 9- or 10-inch spring-form or tube pan. Bake at 350° for 30 minutes; reduce heat to 325° for last 30 minutes. Cool 10 minutes and remove from pan.

Glaze: ½ cup powdered sugar, 1 tbsp. cocoa, ¼ tsp. salt, 2 drops almond extract, 3 tsp. warm water. Decorate with whole blanched almonds.

Jule

All Christmas preparations had to be completed by noon on December 24, Christmas Eve. Shops closed, office workers went home, and soon church bells rang. After Mother's lunch of Christmas breads and her special liver pâté, we started to church. In our village in Jutland (Denmark) the Christmas service was early—at three o'clock. On the way we greeted each other with the happy words, "A blessed feast!" or "A blessed Christmas!"

Meanwhile at home the goose with its stuffing of prunes and apples sizzled in the oven. Red cabbage had been cooked days before (it is best that way), and tiny potatoes, saved for weeks just for this day, were cooked and ready to brown in caramel sauce. Dessert was traditional plain boiled rice pudding sprinkled with cinnamon sugar—not terribly popular the rest of the year, but on this night it all would be eaten, for in someone's portion was hidden an almond, and that *someone* received the "almond gift"—a marzipan (candy) pig.

After dishes were cleared, Father went to the living room to light the candles on the tree while the rest of us waited outside the door in the dark. What a sense of delicious excitement—muffled sounds from within and the smell of spruce twig singed by candle flame.

Then the door was thrown open and we all caught our breath. Each year it seemed unbelievable. We joined hands and walked in a circle around the tree, looking at the well-loved ornaments, the star which Mother had enjoyed as a small girl, the gently flickering candles, while we sang at the top of our voices the Christmas carols practiced since Advent. The custom of walking around the tree is an old pagan rite, perhaps, but the whole reason for Christmas was real enough to everyone as we sat on the floor listening to the story of Jesus' birth.

—*Johanna Reynolds, a former Friends Service worker in China, now living in Hong Kong.*

Nowhere is Christmas celebrated quite so warmly—or with so much light and good food—as in Denmark. On Christmas Eve the most lavish meal of the year is eaten. And after dessert, the plates of cookies and cakes are passed and the coffee pot refilled many times. *Julekage* (Yule-ah-kay-ah) is part of this tradition in Danish homes and in the home of Esther Harvest in Los Gatos, California.

Danish Julekage

1 cup milk	½ cup sugar
2 tbsp. active dry yeast	1 tsp. ground cardamom
4 cups flour	1½ cups raisins and
2 tsp. salt	citron, chopped
⅔ cup sweet butter	Topping
2 eggs	

Scald milk. Set aside; cool to lukewarm. Add yeast and dissolve. Sift 3 cups flour and salt into mixing bowl. With your hand or mixer, crumble butter (may be half margarine) into flour. Beat eggs and sugar with electric mixer. Add milk, yeast, and cardamom. Gradually beat in half the flour and butter mixture. Beat for 5 minutes. Gradually add remaining flour mixture and mix well. Mix in fruit lightly. Turn out onto floured board (using remaining 1 cup flour) and knead until smooth and satiny, 8–10 minutes.

Place in greased bowl, turning to grease top of dough. Cover and set in warm place and let rise until double in bulk (about 4 hours). Punch down; knead lightly. Pat dough into greased 9×13-inch pan. Spread with melted butter. Cover and let rise in warm place until almost double in bulk. Sprinkle with ¼ cup chopped blanched almonds and ¼ cup sugar. Bake at 350° for 30 minutes. Cool. Serve warm.

Come Stir the Pudding!

"Grandmother used to boil our Christmas pudding in the old brick copper (normally used for the weekly wash) in the far corner of her kitchen," remembers Joyce Marsh of Chandlers Ford, England. "Traditional Christmas pudding has to be boiled many hours, so the copper was scrubbed until it gleamed, ready for the long boiling. (This is what makes it so delicious—it's steamed, not baked.)

"There was even a ritual, a kind of folk custom to mixing the batter," says Joyce. "When all the fruits were in, Grandmother called to us, 'Come stir the pudding!' So we all took turns giving it a stir—clockwise, of course, for good luck. A genuine pudding will also have silver coins in it for good fortune. It used to be a threepenny or a Joey.

"Grandma ladled the batter into china basins (molds), tied them in linen cloths, and gently lowered them into the copper. The whole kitchen felt warm and steamy while the pudding cooked.

"The secret of a good plum pudding," Joyce adds, "is the long, slow cooking and the addition of a good spirit which gives it flavor and ensures good keeping. Puddings are sometimes made a month in advance and have been known to be kept a year."

46

STIR UP SUNDAY is the popular name for the Sunday before Advent. By tradition it was the last occasion on which Christmas cakes and puddings could be made if they were to be ready by December 25. It was called Stir Up Sunday after the Collect in the service for that day: "Stir up we beseech thee, O Lord, the wills of thy faithful people . . . ."

∘　∘　∘

Plum pudding began as "plum soup" centuries ago. Originally it was a porridge-like mixture made with mutton, steak, and fruits, including plums. In Old England, it was simply called "Christmas Pudding."

English Christmas Pudding

Plum pudding is the grand finale of every English Christmas. Its pungent fragrance was enough to melt even the heart of Scrooge.

> In half a minute Mrs. Cratchit entered, flushed, but smiling proudly: with the pudding blazing ... and bedight with Christmas holly stuck into the top. "Oh, what a wonderful pudding!" Bob Cratchit said.

1 cup sultanas
1 cup golden raisins
¾ cup currants
½ cup mixed candied fruit, chopped
½ cup slivered almonds
1 medium cooking apple, pared and grated
¼ lb. minced beef suet, chopped
1 tbsp. orange peel, grated
1 tsp. lemon peel, grated

2 cups fresh bread crumbs
1 cup flour
½ cup dark brown sugar
½ tsp. salt
½ tsp. soda
½ tsp. allspice
½ tsp. cinnamon
3 eggs
¼ cup apple cider
2 tbsp. orange juice
2 tbsp. lemon juice
Hard Sauce

Combine sultanas, raisins, currants, candied fruit, almonds, grated apple, suet, orange and lemon peel in a large bowl. Mix bread crumbs, flour, brown sugar, salt, soda, and spices. Stir into fruit mixture. Beat eggs until foamy; add apple juice (or you may use ¼ cup brandy), orange and lemon juices. Stir into fruit mixture. Spoon into a well-greased 1-quart china or glazed pottery mold. Cover top with circle of buttered grease-proof paper next to the pudding. Cover with foil and secure with string.

Place mold on rack in deep kettle; add 1 inch water. Heat water to boiling; reduce heat and cover kettle. Steam about 4-5 hours. Add boiling water to kettle when necessary. Remove mold from kettle. Remove foil; cool on wire rack. Wrap in foil and store in refrigerator at least 3 weeks.

To serve, steam mold on rack in covered kettle with 1 inch boiling water until heated, about 1-2 hours. Remove from kettle; cool slightly and unmold. Decorate and serve with whipped cream or brown sugar hard sauce.

Hard Sauce: Cream 6 tbsp. butter, 6 tbsp. sieved brown sugar until light and fluffy. Beat in 1 tbsp. at a time 2-3 tbsp. cream (or 2-3 tbsp. brandy) and ½ tsp. vanilla. Beat until mixture is light in color and holds shape. Spoon into serving dish. Refrigerate at least 1 hour.

Mincemeat Tartlets

Following the plum pudding at an English Christmas dinner comes a plate piled with hot little mince pies, dusted with sugar. These little tarts always have "lids."

1 cup cooking apples, chopped	⅓ cup brown sugar
1 cup raisins	¼ cup almonds, chopped
½ cup currants	¼ tsp. allspice
½ cup beef suet, chopped fine	¼ tsp. cinnamon
⅓ cup mixed candied fruit, chopped	⅛ tsp. cloves
	⅓ cup apple cider
	Pie crust pastry
	Powdered sugar

Pare, core, and chop apples; combine with raisins, currants, suet, candied fruit, brown sugar, almonds, spices, and apple cider (⅓ cup brandy may be used in place of apple cider) in a large bowl. Cover bowl and set mincemeat in a cool place for 3-4 weeks.

Prepare pie crust pastry and chill. Roll pastry into a circle ⅛ inch thick. Cut 12 circles with 4½-inch cookie cutter. Press circles into well-greased and floured 2½-inch muffin tins, allowing ¼ inch dough above the rim.

Heat oven to 375°. Spoon 3 tbsp. mincemeat into each tart shell. Roll remaining pastry dough ⅛ inch think. Cut 12 circles with 2¾-inch cookie cutter. Place circles over filling. Seal edges and flute. Pierce tops several times with fork. Alternate topping: Cut stars with cookie cutter and fit over tops of tartlets instead of closed tops.

Bake at 375° for about 20 minutes or until crusts are golden. Cool on wire rack. Reheat before serving. Sprinkle lightly with powdered sugar before serving.

Jack Horner pie is named for the Christmas or mince pie from which the nursery rhyme character "took out a plum."

Before the Reformation the traditional shape for mince pies was oblong, representing the crib or manger. Sometimes this was covered with pastry. Puritans found this upsetting and considered it superstitious idolatry.

Dundee Cake

"Boxing day in England is the day the lord and lady of the manor used to wait on their servants and give them money in boxes for Christmas presents," says Joyce Marsh of Chandlers Ford, England. "Now we celebrate the day with a Dundee cake, which is also very traditional but not as rich as the Christmas Cake."

½ cup + 2 tbsp. butter	Rind of 1 lemon, grated
⅔ cup sugar	1¼ cups sultanas or
3 eggs	raisins
2 cups flour	1¼ cups currants
1 tsp. baking powder	¼ cup candied cherries,
2-2½ tbsp. milk	halved
Rind of 1 small orange,	¼ cup candied peel,
grated	diced
	½ cup almonds, ground

Place butter and sugar in mixing bowl and cream until light and fluffy. Add eggs, 1 at a time, beating well after each addition. Gradually blend in sifted flour and baking powder. If mixture seems too dry, add milk. Carefully fold in lemon and orange peel, currants, sultanas or raisins, cherries, candied peel, ground almonds. Spoon into greased 8-inch cake pan lined with greaseproof paper. Arrange almond halves in flower patterns lightly on top of smoothed batter. Bake at 325° for about 2 hours or until the center is firm. Cool in pan. Keeps well in an airtight tin.

Before dawn on Christmas morning, the Scots were up baking cakes called sowens; *one was given to each member of the family. If it did not break, happiness would come to the owner.*

English Christmas Cake

Christmas cake in England is a large, round, rich, dark fruit cake served at tea time on Christmas Day. In the north of England it is covered with a layer of marzipan and perhaps a sprig of holly. In the south it becomes more elaborate with the addition of royal icing and tiny Christmas ornaments.

¾ cup each raisins, currants, and golden raisins

½ cup dried apricots, diced

1 cup fruit cake mix

¼ cup candied lemon and orange peel, diced

½ cup candied red cherries, quartered, (or candied red pineapple, chopped)

½ cup slivered almonds

½ cup butter, softened

½ cup brown sugar

3 eggs

½ cup orange juice

1 tsp. vanilla

½ tsp. each cloves, cinnamon, nutmeg

¼ tsp. soda

½ tsp. salt

1½ cups flour

Apricot jam

Marzipan

Royal icing

Soak diced apricots in warm water until soft; drain and pat dry. In a large bowl combine raisins, golden raisins, currants, fruit cake mix, peel, apricots, cherries, and nuts. Sprinkle with ¼ cup of the sifted flour, tossing to coat evenly. Set aside. Cream butter and sugar until fluffy. Add eggs, one at a time, beating well. Add orange juice (traditionally, 2 tbsp. brandy are part of the liquid), vanilla (omit if using brandy), spices, and mix well. Gradually add remaining flour and soda. Stir in fruit and nuts. Spoon batter into well-greased 8-inch spring-form pan or 8×2 inch cake or pyrex pan lined with grease-proof paper.

Bake at 325° about 70–90 minutes, or until cake tester comes out clean. (To prevent over-browning or drying out, cover lightly with foil, if necessary.) Cool in pan 30 minutes. Remove to cooling rack. Wrap in plastic and foil and store in cool place at least 3 weeks. One week before Christmas brush cake with warm, sieved apricot jam and cover with marzipan. A day before Christmas, cover with royal icing (optional). Cake improves with age and may be stored several months.

Marzipan Covering: Crumble 8–10 oz. good quality almond paste and beat with electric mixer. Add ½ tsp. almond extract, 1 egg yolk, and 1–2 cups sifted powdered sugar. If necessary, knead with hands. On surface sprinkled with sifted powdered sugar, roll out half the marzipan to 8½-inch circle. Roll remaining marzipan into long strip to fit sides of cake. Brush cake with warm, sieved apricot jam. Place marzipan circle on top of cake and gently press into place. Wrap long strip around side of cake, pressing gently to secure. Trim. Wrap cake in foil and one week later frost with royal icing (optional).

Royal Icing: Combine 2 small egg whites, 2–3 tsp. glycerine (this makes icing softer), ½ tsp. lemon juice, and 1½ cups sifted powdered sugar in mixing bowl; beat hard until fluffy. Add additional 1½ cups powdered sugar; beat to stiff mixture. Spread sides and top of cake with thin layer of icing. (Cover bowl with cloth; icing dries quickly.) Remaining icing may be used to pipe decorative edging. Pipe red-tinted holiday greeting on top. Traditionally, small Christmas ornaments, such as trees, are placed on top of cake.

Good recipes are passed from friend to friend. Adaline Karber (San Jose, California) got this fruit cake recipe from her sister-in-law, Mary Martens (British Columbia), who got it from an English friend who got it from . . . !

"We always listen to the Queen's speech on Christmas day," says Joyce Marsh. "We plan our dinner before or after her message. It's tradition in most every British family to listen to her speech."

Night of the "Big Nuff"

"The afternoon of December 24, Mother always served a 'big tea'—little mince pies, rolls, sweets, and tea. We really didn't have many special things during the holidays like the English did," recalls Eithne Cunnane Cuckel of her childhood in County Mayo, Ireland. "We were too poor and didn't have the supplies. My dad called Christmas Eve 'Big Nuff'—the only night you got enough to eat! When he was small, currant buns were a treat—just plain bread with raisins.

"Since ours was a very small village, we didn't have midnight mass. Christmas morning we opened our presents and then were off to church. After dinner we sometimes were too full to cut the Christmas Cake. (p. 58) and saved it until 'Little Christmas' (January 6).

"Our first Christmas tree was very special," recalls Eithne. "An aunt sent us the lights. Making decorations and putting up the tree were all a part of the celebration. Dad built a little stable and crib (créche) for us. When Mother brought it out, we children gathered around for a rosary and carols. My brother Shamus played the piano."

Irish Boiled Fruit Cake

This is our traditional holiday cake, says Eithne Cuckel of Milpitas, California. The recipe comes from my mother, Kathleen Cunnane, who still lives in County Mayo, Ireland.

1 cup margarine	½ cup candied cherries
1 cup dark brown sugar	¼ cup fresh orange
1 cup apple juice or	peel, grated
hot water	½ cup dried fruit,
½ cup prunes, chopped,	chopped
or sultanas	3½ cups flour
1 cup dark raisins	½ tsp. baking soda
1 cup golden raisins	1¼ tsp. allspice
¾ cup currants	1¼ tsp. nutmeg
½ cup dried apricots,	2 eggs, beaten
chopped	¼ cup blanched almonds,
	chopped

Butter a round, 9×3-inch spring-form pan or tube pan and line with greaseproof paper. Place margarine, sugar, apple juice or water (this cake is traditionally made with 1 cup Guinness Stout, in place of water, which enhances the flavor considerably), in a saucepan and bring to a boil, stirring until sugar dissolves and margarine is melted. Add mixed fruits and peel; then simmer over low heat for 3-5 minutes.

Remove from heat and cool to lukewarm. Sift flour, soda, and spices into large bowl. Make a well in center. Beat eggs and add to flour. Add cooled fruit mixture and almonds, mixing well. Turn into prepared tin and smooth top. Bake 1½–2 hours at 325° or until toothpick inserted comes out clean. Brush cake with white Karo syrup while hot and decorate with candied fruits and whole blanched almonds. Cool in tin. Wrap in foil. Store in covered container. Allow to mellow several weeks; cake improves with age.

In one part of Ireland Christmas Eve was called "The Night of the Cakes."

DUMB CAKES—While English men were dragging in the Yule log, women were busy cooking for Christmas Day. A traditional cake for Christmas Eve was the Dumb Cake which was made by single girls who wanted to know who their husbands were going to be. The young lady was forbidden to talk while she made the cake and put it in the oven. Then she was to open the door, and with some good luck, her future husband should walk into the kitchen at the stroke of midnight and turn the cake.

"Four to six weeks before Christmas we made this big basinful of fruit cake," says Marie Martinez, who grew up in Dublin, Ireland. "When all the ingredients were in, everyone had a go around with the spoon—if you could move it!—and made a wish. Later Mum topped the cake with royal icing and some fancy piping around the edge. We decorated the top with small ornaments. It was served at tea time on Christmas Day.

"Before Christmas Eve everyone was busy sprucing up the house. Curtains had to be washed, floors waxed. Dad would go out into the country to get holly and we hung it everywhere— along the wall, on the ledge over the doors, on top of pictures."

Marie's mother always put a two-foot candle in the window on Christmas Eve. According to an old Irish legend, the glow of the candles welcomed the Holy Family, who were said to be traveling the roads of the world. The tiny flickering lights, all over the countryside, invited anyone, who, like Joseph and Mary, might be looking for shelter.

"The day after Christmas—St. Stephen's Day—in Ireland we used to dress up in old rags and go from door to door begging for help to 'bury the wren' (always pronounced *wran*)," says Eithne Cuckel. "We sang, danced, or recited this poem for the lady of the house:

> The wran, the wran, the king of all birds,
> St. Stephen's Day he got caught in the furze (bushes).
> Though he's little, his family is great,
> Cheer up, good lady, and give us a treat!"

An old Irish legend describes a contest between an eagle and a skylark to see which could fly higher. A wren perched on the eagle's back; when the giant bird could fly no longer, the wren took off, soaring far above him.

St. Stephen's Day was called *Wrenning Day*, when they stoned a wren "in commemoration of St. Stephen, the first Christian martyr."

"For Christmas in Finland we always made *Joulotortut* (Yole-o-tor-tu), prune tarts," (p. 63), recalls Terttu Gilbert who grew up on a farm in that country. "The whole family helped Mother shape them in pinwheels and half moons. There was plenty of cutting and filling to be done, for 175 tarts were served to friends who came during the holidays. Mother also made a wreath of *pula*, our sweet bread filled with raisins and cardamom (the Christmas spice), and plenty of little round, spicy cookies called *piparkakut*. Some evenings we sipped hot berry drink made from black currants simmered with raisins, almonds, spices, and orange peel.

"Father usually butchered a pig in December so there was ham for Christmas dinner with prunes, apples, and boiled potatoes along with the traditional rice pudding with a hidden almond. The person finding it might get married that year; or if a young child, that person had to help with the dishes. My brother always swallowed the almond to escape that task.

"There were gifts to make for the whole family—Mother knitted and made dolls. Father built cars from wood for the boys. We made straw decorations for the tree and straw rams (*Joulopässi*) for the tables. Cleaning and baking started early; the house and barn had to be put in a 'Christmas condition.'"

—Terttu Gilbert is a mental health worker in San Jose, California.

Joulotortut
(Finnish Christmas Tarts)

½ lb. pitted prunes
1 cup water
Juice of ½ lemon
1 tsp. lemon rind, grated
¼ cup sugar

1 pkg. (17 oz.) frozen puff pastry° or frozen patty shells

Soak prunes until plump. Simmer in water until very soft. Add water as necessary. Mash to consistency of applesauce. Season with lemon and sugar; increase sugar if necessary.

Thaw 1 sheet puff pastry according to directions. Flour board, rolling pin. Roll pastry ⅛-inch thick. Cut in 4-inch circles, placing circles in refrigerator until ready to fill

Wet edges of circles with water. Spoon 1 tsp. filling on one half of each circle. Fold over. Seal edges with prongs of a fork. Prick pastry. Brush with 1 egg beaten with 1 tbsp. water. Place on baking sheet. Bake at 450° for 8–10 minutes or until brown. Warm before serving.

° Frozen puff pastry sheets are available in frozen food sections of local supermarkets.

"In France we have lovely, religious manger scenes outside the churches. They are so popular that people come from outside of France to see them. Often you must wait in line a long time to see the crèche," recalls Elizabeth Thomas, of San Jose, California.

In Southern France it was the custom for the shepherd of a flock to bring a newborn lamb to the church for blessing on Christmas Eve. This tradition is still carried out at midnight mass in Les Baux (Provence), where men and women dressed as shepherds and shepherdesses form a candlelight procession to the church. A shepherd leads a small ceremonial cart festooned with candles and greenery bearing a white lamb to the altar.

64

Bûche de Noël
(French Christmas Log)

In France it is traditional to have thirteen desserts for Christmas dinner—walnuts, tangerines, dates, etc., but one of them must be the Bûche de Noël. The dessert is shaped like a yule log, filled and frosted with chocolate buttercream.

Cake Roll

6 egg yolks
½ cup sugar
1 tsp. vanilla
¼ tsp. salt

⅔ cup cake flour
½ tsp. baking powder
6 egg whites
¼ tsp. cream of tartar

Mocha Buttercream

1 cup sugar
⅓ cup water
2 eggs
2 tsp. vanilla

3 tsp. instant coffee
4 oz. unsweetened chocolate
1 cup sweet butter

Chocolate Meringue Buttercream

3 egg whites
¼ tsp. cream of tartar
1 cup sugar
⅓ cup water

2 tsp. vanilla
3 tsp. instant coffee
8 oz. semi-sweet chocolate
1 cup sweet butter

Cake Roll for Bûche de Noël: In mixer bowl beat yolks until light. Add sugar gradually and beat until very creamy. Blend in vanilla and salt. Sift cake flour, measure, and sift with baking powder. Gradually fold into egg yolk mixture. Beat whites until foamy; add cream of tartar and beat until stiff but not dry. Fold gently into egg yolk mixture. Spread in jelly roll pan greased and lined with wax paper. Bake at 400° 10–12 minutes or until golden and done. Immediately turn onto damp towel lined with wax paper under it. Peel paper from cake. Roll cake lengthwise in towel and wax paper and let cool at room temperature. Follow directions for constructing the Bûche with *either* mocha buttercream *or* chocolate meringue buttercream.

Mocha Buttercream: Beat eggs until light. Combine sugar and water in small saucepan and cook to soft-ball stage (234°). Beating constantly, gradually add to eggs and beat until cold. Add vanilla and coffee crystals and melted cooled chocolate. Gradually beat in room-temperature butter.

Chocolate Meringue Buttercream: Beat egg whites (room temperature) until foamy; add cream of tartar and beat at high speed until whites form stiff peaks. Combine sugar and water and boil until mixture forms a soft ball (234°). Slowly pour hot syrup into egg white mixture, beating constantly. Beat at high speed for about 5 minutes, until mixture is cool, smooth, and satiny. Beat melted chocolate, coffee, and vanilla into cool meringue. Gradually beat in room-temperature butter. Chill until spreading consistency is reached.

Constructing the Bûche: Unroll cooled cake. Spread with half of the buttercream or meringue buttercream. Roll again and spread most of the remaining buttercream over top and sides. Slicing diagonally, cut off ends of cake. Frost with rest of buttercream and attach to cake to resemble knotholes on log. Use fork to make marks resembling bark across top of cake and knotholes. Decorate with holly leaves and berries made from marzipan (p. 55). Tint as desired with paste food coloring. Dust work surface with powdered sugar and roll marzipan thinly as possible. Cut with sharp knife. Set leaves on log to give three-dimensional effect. (For fluffier buttercream you may use about ⅓ margarine to ⅔ butter.)

Easy Bûche de Noël

Anne Marie Boube, of the French Consulate in San Francisco, loves to do gourmet cooking on weekends. She suggests this log "which is easy and suitable when you have to cook a large meal because it doesn't take long to prepare."

1 lb. tin chestnut purée°	3 tbsp. strong coffee
4 oz. semi-sweet chocolate	6 tbsp. sweet butter
⅔ cup powdered sugar	Powdered sugar
	Whipped cream

Mash chestnut purée to soften. Melt chocolate; add powdered sugar, butter, chestnut purée, and coffee. Mix with wooden spoon until very smooth.

Pour chocolate mixture onto sheet of foil and form into shape of a log. Refrigerate. Place log on serving plate. With prongs of a fork, trace lines to resemble bark of a tree. Sprinkle with powdered sugar to resemble snow. Serve with side serving of whipped cream.

° Imported from France, chestnut purée is available in specialty food stores.

68

The Cake of the Kings

"Our Christmas season in France comes to an end on Epiphany (January 6) when we commemorate the coming of the three kings to Bethlehem," says Elizabeth Thomas. "Everyone celebrates this day—even the schools.

"The special attraction which concludes every Twelfth Night dinner is the *Galette des Rois,* the cake of the kings. Inside the galette is a bean, or good-luck charm called *fève.* The one finding the charm becomes king for the evening and he may choose a queen. We do it at home and the kids love it."

A golden paper crown tops the *galette* when it comes to the table, along with a silver crown for the queen. Often they are made by one of the children in the family. If the cake comes from a bakery, the baker sends the traditional crowns.

In some parts of France, expecially Normandy, children go about singing traditional Twelfth Night carols.

Other countries have similar customs—like the almond in the Christmas Eve rice dish in Scandinavia, the sixpence in the English Christmas pudding, the gold coin in Greek *Vasilopita,* and Mexican families search for a bean or tiny doll in their *Rosca de los Reyes* to bring good fortune.

Galette des Rois

(Cake of the Kings)

From Northern France and Paris comes this cake for Epiphany.
Marthe Nussbaumer of Alsace bakes this almond-filled pastry
for the holiday.

2 eggs
¾ cup powdered sugar
4 tbsp. soft butter
2 tbsp. lemon rind, grated
1 tbsp. lemon juice or kirsch

1 cup + 3 tbsp. ground almonds or filberts, , or 1 cup + 3 tbsp. almond powder, or 1 can (8 oz.) almond paste
Dry bean or fève
Egg glaze

½ pkg. (17-oz.) frozen puff pastry

Thaw puff pastry according to directions. Flour board and rolling pin; roll out. Cut 2 10-inch circles and place 1 circle on baking sheet, flan, or pie pan. Spread filling evenly over pastry,
leaving ¾-inch border. Place bean or fève in any part of paste.
Wet edges of circle with water. Cover filling with top circle of
puff pastry. Seal firmly and crimp edges. Brush with an egg
lightly beaten. With fine point of knife make diamond designs

over top of pastry. Prick dough well with fork prongs. Cover with plastic wrap and chill well. Bake at 400° for 20 minutes. Cool before serving.

Filling: Beat sugar and eggs until thick and lemon-colored. Add butter, ground nuts, or powder, or almond paste, lemon rind, and flavoring. Mix well.

From gold and silver foil or other paper, make crowns for king and queen. Present cake topped with king's crown.

The center of the French Christmas celebration is the crèche, or manger scene. Every home will have its own with tiny clay figures called *santons* (little saints).

After midnight mass on Christmas Eve comes the *réveillon*, the late supper that is the big event of the season. In Alsace, goose is the main dish—in Brittany, buckwheat cakes with sour cream. Burgundy feasts on turkey and chestnuts, while Paris enjoys its *pâté de foie gras*.

Gifts are exchanged at New Year's.

EVERYWHERE IN GERMANY the four weeks of Advent are looked upon as a time of preparation for the greatest festival of the Christian year.

Children happily make their own Christmas greetings, while mothers and grandmothers knit furiously to finish the last mittens, caps, and stockings. Fathers may carve or build toys for young children. And from every kitchen comes the sweet aroma of spicy ginger cookies, cakes, and tortes baking for the big celebration, Christmas Day.

On Sundays, in both homes and churches, Advent wreaths with their four candles are lit, one for each Sunday. In the dusk of the late afternoon families gather around the wreath and the warm fire to play the piano and sing carols. Coffee is served, and Mother proudly brings out the first Christmas cookies for everyone to sample and "see how they turned out."

Christmas Kugelhopf

This delightful holiday cake/bread is traditionally baked in a *Kugelhopf* mold. Decorated with small red candles and holly leaves, it becomes a festive offering for a Christmas brunch or tea. Originating in Austria, *Kugelhopf* (also known as *Gugelhupf* or *Napfkuchen*) is popular in France, Germany, and Switzerland as well.

1 pkg. active dry yeast	1 tsp. salt
½ cup lukewarm water	1 tsp. vanilla
1 tsp. sugar	Grated peel of 1 lemon
1 cup sweet butter, softened	4 cups flour
2/3 cup sugar	1 cup golden raisins
6 eggs	½ cup slivered almonds
	Powdered sugar

Dissolve yeast in warm water and 1 tsp. sugar. Cream butter and sugar; add salt, lemon rind, vanilla, and eggs, one at a time, beating well after each addition. Add yeast mixture and gradually add 2 cups sifted flour. Beat hard with electric mixer for 5 minutes. Gradually add remaining flour and continue beating until dough is elastic. Stir in raisins. Turn into greased bowl; cover with a towel and let rise in warm place until doubled in bulk (about 1½-2 hours). Stir dough down; add almonds. Spoon into well-greased and floured 10-inch *Kugelhopf* mold or tube pan.

Cover and let rise in warm place until batter comes within ½ inch of top of mold (about 1 hour). Bake at 475° for 10 minutes; reduce heat to 350° and continue baking for about 40-45 minutes or until cake tester comes out clean. Let stand in pan 5 minutes before turning out on cooling rack. Before serving, dust with powdered sugar. Decorate with small red birthday-size candles and holders, holly leaves, and berries. Serve warm with fresh butter.

Greek Vasilopita

Baked by every housewife and village baker, this traditional cake honors Basil, the patron saint of the Greek New Year. Decorated with numerals of the coming year and baked with a hidden coin inside, the *Vasilopita* is cut exactly at the stroke of midnight. Aristea Pettis, San Jose, California, shares this recipe from her treasure of Greek cooking.

2 pkg. active dry yeast	2 tsp. orange rind, grated
½ cup warm water	
1 tsp. sugar	2 tsp. mahlep° (optional) or 1 tsp. cardamom
½ cup milk	
¾ cup sugar	½ tsp. salt
⅔ cup butter	5-5½ cups flour
3 eggs	Egg glaze, Sesame seed

Grind the mahlep. Dissolve yeast in warm water and sugar. Heat milk, butter, and ¾ cup sugar over medium heat until dissolved. Pour into large mixing bowl. When lukewarm, add yeast mixture, slightly beaten eggs, orange rind, salt, and spice. Gradually add half the flour and beat 5 minutes with electric mixer. Gradually add 2-2½ cups flour as necessary. Turn out onto lightly floured board and knead until smooth and elastic, about 8–10 minutes. Place in greased bowl, turning to grease top of dough. Cover and set in warm place until double in bulk.

Knead a second time; cover and let rise again. Punch down and return dough to bowl for a *third* rising. Punch down and shape into a round ball, reserving a small piece the size of a lime for decoration. Pat into 10-inch spring-form pan. Cover and let stand in warm place until almost double in bulk.

On floured board, roll small piece of dough into pencil-thin rope, adding extra flour. Cut in 4 pieces and shape numbers of coming year. Lay gently on top of cake. Brush with 1 egg beaten with 1 tbsp. water. Traditionally, the top is sprinkled with black and white sesame seeds (available in Greek delis). Bake at 350° for about 45 minutes or until hollow-sounding when tapped. Makes 1 large loaf. Cut in thirds across loaf and slice in ½-inch pieces.

°Mahlep, a Middle Eastern spice made from the kernel of black cherries, adds fragrance and sweetness to baking. A Greek baker suggests using 1 tsp. ground cardamom or coriander as a substitute. Greek delis carry mahlep.

IN GREECE, gifts are exchanged on St. Basil's Day rather than Christmas, which is a religious celebration. A special cake (p. 76) is baked with a coin inside in remembrance of Basil, who is known for his generosity to the poor. He is said to have helped orphaned and destitute young girls with their dowries by slipping coins into little cakes, then tossing them through the window at night.

New Year's Eve is an important family evening when even the youngest may stay up, joining in games and storytelling until midnight. When church bells chime at twelve o'clock, the father slices the *Vasilopita* (Vas-i-*low*-pita) with pieces for the church, the poor, the eldest in the family, and on down. Pieces are quickly torn apart in search of the coin which brings good luck for the rest of the year.

In some places families take the *Vasilopita* to the church for a priestly blessing before the family gathering.

IN MEXICO children believe the wise men bring their gifts on Three Kings' Day, or Epiphany (January 6). "On that evening children put out water and hay for the wise men's camels," recalls Rosa Cavillo of San Jose, California, "and we set our shoes on the windowsill, hoping for gifts from the kings. The presents were little things—like a brush and comb, or a bracelet, but they were very special to us.

"Mother baked the traditional Three Kings' Cake (p. 80) in the shape of a ring or crown which she used as a centerpiece for our big dinner. The honor of cutting the cake went to my grandmother."

Inside the cake is a small china doll or bean. The person finding it becomes king or queen for the meal, but that person is also obligated to host a party or supper on Candlemas, February 2. Sometimes the finder, not feeling quite so lucky, quickly swallows the bean.

Mexican Rosca de los Reyes

Three Kings' Cake is a fruit and nut filled ring or crown topped with icing and decorations. It is traditional for Three Kings' Day in Mexico.

2 pkgs. active dry yeast	1 tsp. orange peel, grated
½ cup lukewarm water	4–5 cups flour
1 tsp. sugar	½ cup raisins
⅔ cup milk	½ cup candied orange peel, chopped
4 tbsp. butter	¼ cup candied red and green cherries, chopped
¼ cup sugar	½ cup walnuts, chopped
½ tsp. salt	Glaze
3 eggs	
1 tsp. lemon peel, grated	

Dissolve yeast and sugar in warm water. Over medium heat, warm milk, butter, sugar, and salt. Cool to lukewarm. Beat eggs until light. Add orange and lemon peel, milk and yeast mixtures to eggs. Gradually add 2½ cups flour. Beat 5 minutes with electric mixer. Add 1-1½ cups flour, as necessary. Turn out onto floured board and knead until smooth and elastic, about 8–10 minutes. Carefully work in fruit and nuts, distributing evenly. Place in greased bowl, turning to grease top of dough. Cover and let rise in warm place until double in bulk. Punch down.

On lightly floured surface, divide dough in half, roll into 2 26-inch ropes. Form ring and seal ends together. Place on greased baking sheet. Cover and let rise until almost double. Bake at 375° for 10 minutes. Cover with foil and bake 10–15 minutes more. Cool. Cut triangular wedge from cake ring and insert bean or tiny doll. Replace wedge. Glaze with mixture of powdered sugar, cream, and vanilla. Decorate with candied fruits and walnut halves. Sometimes in Mexico glazed orange slices are used as decoration.

Light Christmas Cake from Warsaw

5 eggs	½ tsp. salt
2 cups confectioners' sugar	¼ cup candied orange rind, diced
1 cup butter	½ cup prunes, diced
3 tsp. lemon peel, grated	½ cup figs or dates, diced
1 tsp. vanilla	¾ cup walnuts, chopped
¼ cup orange juice	¾ cup currants or raisins
3 cups cake flour	
2 tsp. baking powder	

Prepare fruit and nuts. Sprinkle with 2 tbsp. of the flour; sift remaining flour with baking powder and salt. Beat eggs until light and lemon-colored. Cream butter, lemon peel, and vanilla until fluffy. Beat in orange juice, eggs and mix. Gradually add flour mixture and beat well. Fold in fruit and nuts. Turn batter into generously greased and floured 10–inch tube pan (or two 8×4×3–inch loaf pans). Bake at 350° 1 hour or until cake tester comes out clean. Cool cake in pan 10 minutes; turn onto wire rack. Spread with lemon glaze.

Lemon Glaze: 1 cup powdered sugar, 2 tbsp. lemon juice, ½ tsp. grated lemon peel mixed.

A Polish Christmas Eve (Wigilia) Supper

Early in the day the father brings in clean straw to lay under the white tablecloth—a reminder of Christ's stable. Mother sets out her best dishes and sets an extra place for an unexpected guest. Polish people believe a guest in the home is God in the home. Food is ready and waiting in the kitchen. Excitement fills the cozy, warm home.

When finally the first star appears in the evening sky, the father calls his family to share the *oplatek* (holy bread of love), a wafer blessed by the priest. Happy is their time together, sharing the twelve special Christmas dishes, singing, and storytelling around the table until the church bells ring at 11:00. Then father readies horses and sleigh for the family to attend mass—the shepherd's watch.

It is the belief in some villages that while the congregation prays, peace descends on the snow covered earth and the humble animals, at home in the barn, are given the power to speak—but only the innocent of heart may hear them.

—From remembrances of Vera Kawulka, Santa Clara, California.

Ukrainian Christmas Eve Supper

Kutya
Marinated Herring
Herring in Tomato Sauce

Fish in Aspic
Baked Stuffed Pike

Christmas Eve Borsch
Vushka (Dumplings with Mushroom Filling)

Sauerkraut with Peas
Holubtsi (Stuffed Cabbage) with
Rice and Mushrooms
Holubtsi (stuffed cabbage) with Buckwheat Kasha
Mushroom Sauce

Varenyky with Sauerkraut Filling
Varenyky with Prune Filling
Compote of Dried Fruit
Christmas Pastries
Pampushky (Doughnuts), Medivnyk (Honey Cake)
Chrusty (Thin Crullers)

Ukrainian Medivnyk

(Honey Cake)

Honey cakes are very much a part of the Ukrainian and Polish Christmas tradition. Lil Proceviat, Mountain View, California, shares her recipe for the true honey lover. Lil prefers the cake plain, enjoying the flavor and aroma of the honey. For best results, she suggests using only buckwheat or a dark, high quality honey. This is a beautiful, light cake.

6	eggs	2	tsp. baking soda
1	cup sugar	¼	tsp. salt
1	cup buckwheat honey	1	tsp. cinnamon
1	cup safflower oil	1	tsp. cloves
1	cup buttermilk	3	cups flour

Beat eggs until light and lemon-colored. Add sugar gradually and mix well. Add honey and oil; cream thoroughly. Combine buttermilk and soda; add to mixture and beat well. Add spices, salt, and gradually add sifted flour. Pour into a well-greased and floured tube or bundt pan. Bake at 350° 1½ hours or until done. Cool 10 minutes in pan and remove to rack. (½ cup chopped walnuts and ⅜ cup chopped raisins may be added to the batter after the addition of flour, if you wish.) Cake stored in airtight container improves with age. May be served with whipped cream.

IN THE UKRAINE the Christmas celebration begins when the first star appears in the evening sky, says Marie Halun Bloch. Usually the children watch for it and call out, "There's the Christmas star!"

Before we sat down to the Christmas Eve meal, my father had prepared black bread sliced very thin and spread with comb honey. Starting with my Mother, he stood in front of her and made a little speech of Christmas wishes. He mentioned all the things he hoped would happen for Mother during the coming year. Then Mother made a little speech to Father and they kissed each other and took a slice of bread and honey. Father did this for each of the children. The younger ones always kissed his hand and gave him a hug before eating their bread.

Mother's table was festive with straw under the embroidered

cloth in remembrance of the manger. A place was set at the table for missing family members or an unexpected guest. Sometimes in rural areas a sheaf of wheat was brought in. Family members considered it an abode for the spirits of ancestors, who, it was believed, returned twice a year to check on their welfare.

Traditionally there were twelve courses at the meal, symbolizing the twelve apostles. However, the most important place at the table was given to a large bowl of *kutya*, made of whole grain wheat boiled with poppy seeds, nuts, figs, dates, and honey. No table was complete without this dish for it signified a plentiful harvest. Everyone took a spoonful of *kutya* and of the other twelve dishes as well. Everything one did at Christmas symbolized the ancient birthday.

Ours was a quiet, thoughtful meal, remembering Christmases past. When we had finished everyone joined in singing carols. There was no visiting on Christmas Eve and no emphasis on gifts. At midnight the family went to the candlelight church service that sometimes lasted three or four hours.

On Christmas Eve a lighted candle was placed in the window an invitation to any homeless stranger to join in celebrating the birth of Christ.

—Marie Halun Bloch, Denver, Colorado, is the author of seventeen books for children. She has written of a childhood Christmas in her book, Marya.

Index

FESTIVE

Cookies

of

CHRISTMAS

For centuries, women all over the world have baked cookies to celebrate the event of Christmas.

Here is a small collection of recipes gathered from friends whose roots go back to fourteen different countries. Many of the cookies are simple—even rather plain, but they are among the most traditional and are still baked in those countries. Where possible, the foreign name of the recipe has been retained to provide a sense of the past.

May these lovely old traditions and recipes enrich your Christmas celebration.

To my dear sister and her daughter—
Yvonne and Laura Dunn—who love to
bake cookies together

Special thanks to cookie enthusiasts Liz Spears, Anne Hyrne, Adaline Karber, Mary Koyama, and Virginia Sharp for testing recipes; to Ruth Capper, Helen Epp, LaDonna Bontrager (Amish), Catherine Weidner (Moravians); the Austrian Consulate of New York City; Marthe Nussbaumer (Alsace); Ester Harvest and Johanna Reynolds (Denmark); Terttu Gilbert (Finland); Doris Walter and Magdalena Meyer (Germany); Aristea Pettis (Greece); Johanna Hekkert and Jan Gleysteen (Holland); Jeannie Bertucelli Snyder, Edith Bertucelli, and Matilde Oliverio (Italy); Rosa Calvillo and Elma Voth (Mexico); Vera Kawulka (Poland); Dr. Ingrid Gamstorp, Margaret Carlsen, and Brigetta Kellgrin (Sweden); Doreen Leith (Scotland); and Lily Gyger (Switzerland), for helpful contributions.

"Finally, it was Christmas Eve. At dinner everybody tried to pretend nothing was particularly special. But everything was. The food tasted more delicious, the air smelled fresher, sweeter; sounds came at a higher pitch; sights seemed sharper, colors richer. It was the same house we lived in all those other 364 evenings, the same rooms, the same furniture, the same stairs, the same people, and yet they seemed now somehow different, transformed."

—Philip Kundhart, Jr., *My Father's House* (New York: Random House).

Of Lebkuchen, Springerle, and Ammonia Cookies

In my childhood home, mother had a few of her own special cookie recipes which she quietly and courageously baked every Christmas despite the fact that her daughters thought them quite dull.

These old recipes for *Lebkuchen, Springerle* (pages 128 and 136), and Ammonia Cookies, gathered from Canadian friends, were penned into a handwritten cookbook with fond memories of visits and warm hospitality.

Mom packed her yearly cookie cache high on a cupboard shelf. But she need not have. Not once did we disturb that box. We much preferred to pilfer gumdrop peppernuts and peanut brittle.

Only in recent years have I discovered, with much chagrin, the lovely delicacy of those Old World cookies—the soft, chewy texture of *Lebkuchen*, the gentle hint of anise in *Springerle*, and experimented with that old-fashioned leavening of our grandmothers, bakers' ammonia.

And wouldn't you know! When I offer these gems at Christmas, my son, with that same maddening aloofness, passes over my discovery for everyday chocolate chip cookies and fudge brownies. Guess who's chuckling now!

94

Moravian Christmas Cookies

"My mother, Lula Brandon, gave me this recipe (p. 96) which I am sure came from her mother," writes Cathcrine Weidner, of Bethlehem, Pennsylvania. "Every year mother made up the dough just after Thanksgiving. Baking day was great fun for the whole family and was often done in the early evening so everyone could help.

"Mother took a small lump of dough and rolled and rolled to get it as thin as possible. My four sisters and I each had a job— placing cookies on a tin, watching the oven, removing the baked cookies to cool, stacking cookies by shape in big lard tins to store until Christmas. . . . The aroma was wonderful. Mother made these cookies every year until she died at 89.

"Moravian cutters, handed down from mother to daughter, come in all shapes and sizes—stars, angels, trees, leaves, hearts, bells, candles, boys, girls, animals, or birds. Some are so tiny they are hardly a bite. I prize highly those from my mother."

Antique Moravian cutters can be found in the Moravian museum in Bethlehem. A few patterns appear on page 97.

Organist, musician, and pastor's wife, Catherine Weidner enjoys a full schedule of church work and entertaining in her home.

Mrs. Henry Brandon's Moravian Christmas Cookies

Mrs. Brandon's daughters bake these cookies by the hundreds for their families and grandchildren. The recipe is much in demand for its lovely combination of molasses and spices, complemented by the subtle flavor of orange. The dough can be rolled to "tissue paper thin."

1 cup dark molasses	1 tbsp. orange extract
1⅓ cups brown sugar, packed	½ tsp. ginger
¼ cup + 2 tbsp. lard or shortening	½ tsp. cinnamon
1½ tsp. soda	½ tsp. cloves
2 tbsp hot water	½ tsp. mace
	4-5 cups flour

Combine molasses, sugar, lard, and soda dissolved in 2 tbsp. hot water over low heat. Melt and cool. Add orange extract. Gradually add flour sifted with spices. Dough should be firm. Mix and knead thoroughly. Cover well and set in cool place to ripen.

Roll small amounts of dough to paper thinness on well-floured, cloth-covered board. Cut into shapes with floured cutters. Place on greased tins, smoothing out any air bubbles. Bake at 350° until light brown. Watch carefully. Store in airtight container.

(Mrs. Brandon used "Puerto Rico Molasses." She also used lard in the dough which makes the cookies flaky and crisp.)

Old Cookie Cutters

Some of the finest early cookie cutters were produced in the Pennsylvania Dutch country where bright colors, ornamentation, and good food inspired the tinsmith.

Designs came from the tinworker's surroundings and he turned out patterns of horses, birds, stars, flowers, hearts, among many others. Cutters were shaped from freehand drawings and frequently were made just before holidays. Many families had one member who could turn out their patterns.

Early cutters were usually made of strong, thin steel plate generously coated with tin. The older the cutter, the deeper the cutting edge. Holes were stamped in the back to allow air to escape when the cutter was pressed into the dough.

Antique cutters were often signed by the tinsmith, dated, and numbered. Recently one rare cutter, nearly a hundred years old, sold for $1,025 at an auction!

A few craftsmen who are reviving this old art and handcraft, sign, date, and number their cutters just as the old tinsmiths did earlier.

Old-Fashioned Sugar Cookies

"My rolled cookie recipe comes from a small bakery run by a Slavic lady who was a friend of our family. I have done almost everything with the dough but walk on it and never had a failure!" says Ruth Capper, Dellroy, Ohio. Here is a trusty recipe to cut into stars, trees, and bells for children to decorate.

1 cup butter	1 tsp. baking powder
1 cup sugar	½ tsp. salt
2 eggs	1 tsp. nutmeg
1½ tsp. vanilla	(optional)
½ tsp. soda	3-3½ cups flour

In a mixing bowl, beat butter until creamy. Beat in sugar, eggs, and vanilla, mixing well. Sift dry ingredients and gradually add to creamed mixture. Beat well. Cover and chill overnight. Roll out dough to ⅛-inch thickness on well-floured board. Cut into favorite designs.

Place on greased baking sheet and bake at 350° for 5-7 minutes or until lightly browned. Cool immediately on racks. Decorate as desired. Makes about 4 dozen cookies.

"I remember my grandmother baking big molasses cookies in her grassburner oven," says Helen Epp, author of *A Treasury of Cookie Recipes*. "She made a fire with bundles of prairie grass. When it had burned down and the coals were just right, she put the cookies on black pans that were exactly the width of the oven. How she knew when the temperature was right, I don't know.

"Grandmother used her own homemade molasses and flour ground from their own wheat. How we loved the smell of those cookies. That was my first lesson in cookie baking."

For the Love of a Cookie!

Ruth Capper has collected cookie cutters for years. But it's not only the cutters Ruth likes, it's the cookie baking as well—especially for her favorite project, the annual Dellroy Historical Society Festival.

During this three-day gala, Ruth and several helpers bake about 3,000 gingerbread boys from an old family recipe. She bakes nonstop from 8:00 in the morning to 6:00 in the evening "on an old stove like mother's, so our cookies are very homemade.

"It's so interesting to see grown men stand in line just to get a warm cookie," says Ruth. "Several remarked they had never eaten a gingerbread boy before and surely never one that had been baked before their own eyes.

"We didn't always have time to decorate the cookies, and one little boy stood a long time looking at his plain cookie. He finally asked, 'Where are the eyes?' When I told him the boy was asleep, he seemed satisfied."

Ruth Capper is president of the national Cookie Cutter Collector's Club. (Yes, there really is such an organization!) She works as secretary, loves gardening, baking, and her role of busy farmer's wife as well.

Chocolate-Covered Pretzels

In the Amish/Mennonite community of Yoder, Kansas, LaDonna Bontrager is known for the good, country-style food she serves in her little *Koffa Haus* (coffeehouse). At Christmas she is lauded for the gallons of peppernuts, cookies, and chocolate-covered pretzels she turns out in her large farm home kitchen. Big trays of these goodies are served to family and friends throughout the holiday season.

Place 6 oz. *coating chocolate* or semi-sweet chocolate chips in top of double boiler over hot, not boiling, water. Add 1 tbsp. shortening or *paramount crystals*. Stir until mixture begins to melt. Remove from heat and stir until completely melted. Coatings dip best at 85°. Dip each pretzel in coating.

Remove with tongs and lay on baking sheets lined with waxed paper. Chill, uncovered, until coating is set. Stack and store in airtight containers. Makes 4-5 dozen.

To achieve professional-looking results, use dark or white *coating chocolate,* which is available in some cake decorating and candy stores or at candy counters in some department stores.

Cherry Chocolate Chippers

For the chocolate chip cookie lover, here is the ultimate Christmas combination enhanced by maraschino cherries.

¾ cup margarine
1 cup brown sugar
1 egg
1 tsp. vanilla
2¼ cups flour
1 tsp. baking powder
½ tsp. salt

6 oz. semi-sweet
    chocolate chips
½ cup chopped nuts
½ cup shredded
    coconut (optional)
½ cup chopped
    maraschino cherries

Cream sugar and margarine until light and fluffy. Add egg and vanilla and beat well. Gradually add flour sifted with baking powder and salt. Mix thoroughly. Gradually add chocolate, nuts, coconut (optional), and then carefully fold in the cherries. Mix lightly. Drop by spoonfuls onto ungreased baking sheet. Bake at 350° for 10-12 minutes. Makes about 12 dozen.

CHRISTMAS at Grandmother Jost's meant dozens of cousins filling that big white frame house at the end of Main Street in Hillsboro. It was a day of laughter, giggling, and games of hide and seek. At dinner, we cousins sat crammed elbow to elbow, at the long oak table in the kitchen, eating ham, *Zwieback, Pluma Moos,* and grandma's spicy, hard peppernuts.

However, the fun ended abruptly when one of the aunts marshaled us into the living room to perform. Who can forget that room with its slightly stuffy smell (it wasn't heated every day) and grandparents sitting primly in front of the bay window, bright with white lace curtains, a flowering Christmas cactus, and spindly geraniums in tin cans. Aunts and uncles sat in straight-back chairs around the room.

We children stood in a line, slightly embarrassed, trying not to giggle, and looking hard at the floor while taking turns reciting the verses we had learned at church. Uncles and aunts nodded, smiling approval. Grandmother more than rewarded our sing-song efforts with little gifts and sacks of nuts and candy. Grandfather gave us each a dime. Those were Christmases with roots, and family, and memories.

We always knew Christmas was coming when mother got out our book of *Wünschen* (wishes). The cover had a pale pastel design, tied with bright yarn. Poems and verses, all handwritten, filled the book. There were shorter poems for the littler children and longer ones for those who were older. I remember some with six or seven verses. These we memorized to recite two or three times—first on Christmas morning for our parents and then again for grandparents at family gatherings. *(Bertha Fast Harder, Elkhart, Indiana)*

Helen Epp recalls learning these Christmas poems for her country school programs. "Sometimes you learned more than one," she says. "The longer the poems, the more you could say and recite, the smarter you were!"

Stained-Glass Windows

A cookie as pretty as a picture—and good to eat, too. The colorful stained-glass effect is easily achieved with hard colored candies.

Eugene Valasek, Canton, Ohio, designed and crafted a special cutter for this cookie for the 1980 Cookie Cutter Collector's Convention.

½ cup sugar	2 cups flour
⅓ cup margarine	2 tbsp. milk
1 egg	10-12 rolls candy,
½ tsp. vanilla	assorted colors
¼ tsp. salt	large silver dragées
1 tsp. baking powder	¼ cup light corn syrup

Cream sugar and margarine until light and fluffy; beat in egg, vanilla, and salt. Gradually add flour sifted with baking powder. Alternate with milk. Chill overnight or until dough handles easily.

Flour pastry cloth or board and rolling pin. Roll out small amounts of dough to ⅛-inch thickness. Dip special stained-glass cutter in flour, cut dough, and gently ease cookie onto foil-lined cookie sheet. Tap lightly until dough drops out.

With toothpick or pointed object, gently lift out cutouts, including hanging holes.

Outline each triangle with about 15 dragées. Break candies (Lifesavers) in half. Into each star cutout place ½ piece yellow candy, into each heart ½ piece red candy, into each triangle ½ piece green candy. (Triangles are not quite as large; you may need a little less, as candy may cook over.) You may also need to substitute colors.

Bake at 350° for 5-7 minutes, until all candies are melted. Watch closely. Cool *completely* on cookie sheet on wire rack. *Peel* foil from cookies. Repeat with remaining cookies. Makes about 1 dozen. (Small cutouts baked separately make delightful refreshments for a dolls' tea party.) Bring corn syrup to boiling over medium heat for 2 minutes. Brush corn syrup evenly over each cookie.

Adaline Karber, San Jose, California, baked enough of these cookies to decorate a Christmas tree for her church.

Lacy Pecan Wafers

Blending flavors of carmel and pecan, these candy-like cookies go well with ice cream or may be filled with whipped cream for an elegant dessert.

⅔ cup ground pecans	1 tbsp. flour
⅓ cup sugar	2 tbsp. milk
½ cup butter	½ tsp. vanilla

Combine all ingredients in a skillet over medium heat and cook until blended. Keep warm. Drop batter (it will be thin) by tea-spoonfuls about 3 inches apart, on well-greased sheet. Allow only 4 or 6 cookies to each pan. Bake at 350° for 5 minutes. Cool on baking sheet 1 minute. Working quickly, remove cookie with spatula, turn over and curl around handle of wooden spoon.

If cookies become brittle, return to oven 1 minute to soften. Cool. Store in airtight container or they may become soft. Makes about 32.

Meringue Kisses

This easy cookie makes an attractive addition to a Christmas gift box or cookie tray.

2 egg whites	6 oz. mini chocolate chips
¾ cup powdered sugar	or ½ cup chopped nuts (walnuts, pecans, or filberts)

Bring egg whites to room temperature. Beat egg whites until foamy. Continue beating while adding sifted sugar gradually. Beat until very stiff. Fold in chocolate bits or nuts. Drop by rounded teaspoonfuls onto parchment-lined cookie sheet. Place in 350° oven and turn off heat immediately. Without opening the door, leave the meringues in oven for at least 6 hours or overnight.

Store in airtight container. Add to cookie gift boxes at the last minute as meringues do not keep well. This recipe makes 2½-3 dozen.

Adaline Karber's Pecan Crisps

Adaline Karber loves to bake—cookies, cakes, breads—with wedding cakes and catering receptions her specialty. While testing recipes for this book, she created an original of her own—Pecan Crisps—a delicate light cookie with the continental flavoring of orange flower water.

½ cup sweet butter
2 tbsp. sugar
1½ cups cake flour

1 tsp. orange flower
water° or
2 tsp. vanilla
¾ cup chopped pecans

Beat butter and sugar until creamy. Add orange flower water. Gradually add sifted cake flour and beat well. Gently mix in nuts; do not overbeat. Roll dough into balls smaller than a walnut and place on parchment-lined baking pan. Press balls down very lightly with a water glass. Bake at 300° for 15 minutes. Cookies should be firm but not brown. Makes 2½ dozen.

° Used frequently in France and the Middle East, *orange flower water* is made from the blossom of Alpine French Riviera Bitter Orange trees. Its delicate flavor enhances cakes, pastries, cream, crepes, candies, and waffles. (Strength and quality may vary.)

Alsatian Schokolade Kugeln
(Chocolate Balls)

Rich and chocolatey, crusty on the outside, soft and moist inside—these chocolate balls are a tradition in Marthe Nussbaumer's French/Alsatian kitchen.

2 eggs
½ cup + 3 tbsp. sugar
4 oz. unsweetened
  chocolate, grated
½ tsp. cinnamon

1 tsp. vanilla
5 tbsp. + 1 tsp. flour
2 cups + 6 tbsp. ground
  almonds
Powdered sugar

Beat eggs and sugar until light and fluffy. Add remaining ingredients and beat well. Pat into a ball and chill in refrigerator at least 1 hour. With a teaspoon, spoon out small balls of dough about ¾ inch in diameter. Roll each in sifted, powdered sugar.

Place on greased baking sheet and allow to dry 4-5 hours in warm kitchen. Bake at 475° for 3-5 minutes. Cool 10 minutes on baking pan and remove to cooling racks. Balls will have light outer crust and soft centers. Makes about 60 balls.

Marthe Nussbaumer's Dukatentaler

Tasty French, Alsatian, and Swiss baking all blend in Marthe Nussbaumer's large farm kitchen near Altkirch (Alsace), France. *Dukatentaler* are from her Christmas collection.

½ cup + 1½ tsp. sweet
   butter
½ cup sugar
2 eggs
1 tsp. vanilla or
   ½ tsp. vanilla sugar

2 cups + 3 tbsp.
   flour
¼ tsp. baking powder
Chocolate Filling
Chocolate Glaze

Beat butter until creamy. Beat in sugar, eggs, and vanilla. Add flour sifted with baking powder to cream mixture. Knead until light and shiny. Chill overnight. Roll to ¼-inch thickness on well-floured board. Cut in dollar-sized circles and place on greased baking sheet. Bake at 350° for about 5 minutes or until lightly browned. Cool on wire racks.

Spread half the circles with Chocolate Filling. Cover with top circle. Glaze ½ of top circle of each cookie with Chocolate Glaze. Makes about 5 dozen double cookies.

Chocolate Filling: 4 tbsp. butter, ½ cup powdered sugar, 1 tsp. vanilla, 1 egg yolk, beaten, 2 oz. unsweetened chocolate, melted. Cream butter. Beat in sugar, vanilla, and egg yolk. Melt chocolate over double boiler and add to mixture. Beat until smooth.

Chocolate Glaze: Mix together ½ cup powdered sugar, 2 tbsp. cocoa, 5 tsp. boiling water, ¼ tsp. vanilla.

A duke in Venice once owned a mint where they made Dukats, *coins named after the owner.*

Originating in Bohemia, the Taler *was minted in* Joachimstal *(Joachim's Valley), and the coin took on the name of* Joachimstaler. *Our English word, dollar, comes from the German* Taler.

Someone, somewhere along the way combined these two words to name this buttery, dollar-sized cookie with a rich chocolate filling. It, too, may be worth its weight in gold.

Family Secrets

In Austrian homes, Christmas begins the Saturday before Advent. In the household of Baroness Maria Von Trapp (whose story was told in "The Sound of Music"), the whole family trooped out to the woods to gather fresh evergreen boughs for their Advent wreath. Around the warmth of a crackling fire in the living room, they tied the fresh, fragrant branches onto a large old wagon wheel. Four white candles, one for each week of Advent, were added. Then the big wreath was hung from the ceiling, suspended by four strong red ribbons.

After supper came time for festive ceremony—lighting the first candle, singing, and prayers. Mrs. Von Trapp brought out a bowlful of cards on which were written the names of the different members of the household. In greatest secrecy, each drew a name and then tossed the card into the fire. From that moment until Christmas, each person had another "in his special care," doing as many little favors and services as possible for that person.

This lovely old custom created a real atmosphere of helpfulness, charity, and true Christmas spirit, remembers Baroness Von Trapp. (Adapted from "Christmas with the Trapp Family," by Greta Sciutto and Margaret Thompson, *In the Very Name of Christmas* [Boston: Chapman & Grimes, Inc.].)

115

Austrian Vanille Kipferl
(Vanilla Crescents)

One bite calls for another of these butter-rich cookies dipped in vanilla sugar.

1 cup butter	1 cup ground blanched
½ cup sugar	almonds
2 egg yolks	½ cup vanilla sugar
3 cups flour	

Cream butter and sugar until light and fluffy. Add egg yolks and beat well. Add sifted flour, ½ cup at a time. Add almonds and continue beating. Refrigerate—not more than 1 hour.

Roll into pencil-thin strips. Cut in 3-inch lengths; turn ends to form crescent. (For consistent shapes, the *Kipferl* may be shaped around a glass or bottle.) Place on lightly greased baking sheet. Bake at 350° for 12-15 minutes or until golden brown. Roll in vanilla sugar mixture. Store in airtight container.

Vanilla sugar is made by placing a vanilla bean or empty vanilla bean pod in a closed jar with sugar for 2-3 days.

Austrian Hussar Rounds

Hussar (*hoo*-zahr) was the name given to the elite division of the Hungarian light cavalry of the 15th century. *Rounds* may refer to their ammunition or bullets. But cookies by this name are quite the opposite—soft, buttery, and light!

1 cup softened butter	3-3½ cups flour
½ cup + 2 tbsp. sugar	1 egg white
2 tbsp. grated lemon peel	Coarsely chopped blanched almonds
½ tsp. vanilla	Apricot jam
3 egg yolks, beaten	Powdered sugar

Cream butter and sugar until fluffy; add lemon peel and vanilla. Add egg yolks alternately with spoons of flour. Mix well. Work in remaining flour until dough is firm and smooth. Pinch off small pieces of dough and roll into 1-inch balls. Make indentations on top of each cookie. Brush with egg white beaten with 1 tbsp. water. Roll each cookie in almonds.

Place on greased baking sheet. Bake at 350° 20-25 minutes or until delicately browned. Cool. Before serving place dab of apricot jam in center. Serve dusted with powdered sugar. Makes about 4 dozen.

Austrian Ischler Tartlets

A seductive flavor duo of almonds and raspberries will call for more than seconds. *Ischler Tartlets* originate in the area of Bad Ischl.

2 cups flour	½ cup sugar
1 cup ground blanched almonds	Raspberry jam
	Chocolate Glaze
1 cup sweet butter	Blanched almond halves

Combine flour and ground almonds in a bowl; work in butter as for pie dough. Blend in sugar. Knead until smooth and dough holds together well. Chill. Roll small portions of dough to ⅛-inch thickness between sheets of waxed paper. Cut with 2-2½-inch round biscuit cutter.

Place on greased baking sheet and bake at 350° for 8-10 minutes or until light golden in color. Remove to racks and cool. When ready to serve, place cookies together in pairs with jam in center. Frost top cookie with Chocolate Glaze. Top with almond half.

Chocolate Glaze: Melt 4 oz. semi-sweet chocolate and 1 tbsp. butter over low heat; beat until smooth. Spread tops of cookies.

Austrian Coconut Macaroons

A hint of fresh lemon makes this a special treat.

2-⅔ cups fresh coconut,
  peeled and shredded°
1 cup sugar
1 egg white
1 tbsp. grated lemon peel

2 tbsp. lemon juice,
  strained
3 egg whites
3 tbsp. flour

Combine coconut, sugar, 1 egg white, lemon peel, and lemon juice in medium saucepan, stirring over low heat until luke-warm. Remove from heat and cool. Beat remaining egg whites until they form soft peaks. Gradually fold egg whites into cooled coconut mixture. Add flour gradually and combine gently.

Place heaping teaspoons of mixture at 1½-inch intervals on well-greased baking sheet. Bake at 275° for about 20-25 minutes or until golden brown. Makes 3 dozen.

°You may substitute commercial coconut.

Linzer Tartlets

Reminiscent of Linzer torte, these special cookies combine filberts, raspberries, and a chocolate glaze for a marvelous flavor treat.

½ cup flour
½ cup sifted bread
   or cake crumbs
⅔ cup ground filberts
⅔ cup butter

⅓ cup sugar
2 tbsp. unsweetened
   chocolate, grated
Raspberry jam
Chocolate Glaze

Combine flour, crumbs, and filberts in a bowl; work in butter. Blend in sugar and chocolate. Knead dough until it holds together. Chill. On floured board, roll small portions of dough to ⅛-inch thickness. (Dough may be slightly crumbly.) With 2-inch biscuit cutter, cut in circles and place on ungreased baking sheet. Bake at 325° for 10-12 minutes or until cookies are firm. Cool on wire racks.

Before serving, place cookies together in pairs with jam in center. (Apricot jam is a good alternate.) Ice with Chocolate Glaze, p. 113. Makes about 1½ dozen double cookies.

A Dutch Saint Nicholas Eve Party

CHOCOLADE LETTER (Chocolate Letters)

SPECULAAS (Cookies)

SPRITS (Letter Cookies)

PEPERNOTEN (Peppernut Cookies)

MARSEPEIN (Marzipan)

BORSTPLAAT (Sugar Candies)

CHOCOLADE MELK (Hot Chocolate)

BANKETLETTER (Saint Nicholas Letter)

ST. NICHOLAS DAY in Holland (December 6) is a time of great fun and merriment for all. "Excitement begins to build as soon as the good saint arrives in town, usually a few days early," recalls Johanna Hekkert of her childhood in the Netherlands. "As soon as he is known to be around, the children set out their shoes at night with treats for his horse, hoping for a small present in return. In the morning, on the way to school, they love to brag about what Sinterklaas left for them."

The big evening is December 5 when the whole family and their closest friends gather to welcome a visit from St. Nicholas. "Suddenly there is a loud knock at the door and a black hand reaches in, tossing *Pepernoten* (tiny cookies) across the floor. That's *Swarte Piet* (Black Peter), his helper, who accompanies him everywhere. The children scramble to see who can pick up the most cookies," says Johanna.

Then the father, or the head of the house, invites St. Nicholas into the living room, asking him to sit in the best chair. The children stand around, looking up at this stately man in his long robe and bishop's miter, listening anxiously as he reads from a book in which everyone's good and bad deeds are recorded. Good children get presents, of course, and for those who need improvement, *Swarte Piet* has a birch switch to encourage better behavior.

"In our home we always exchanged surprises on this evening. Gifts were disguised to make the final discovery more delightful. A small box might be wrapped many times inside a huge unwieldy box, or little things were hidden inside a vegetable or in the pudding. Clues written in poetry often led to a big box somewhere in the cellar. Or perhaps the doorbell rang and there was a present on the steps outside, but there was no one in sight.

"When all the gifts were opened and the poems read, mother served *Speculaas* and hot chocolate. We each got our initials in solid chocolate—mine was a *J*. Often dad would buy a *Banketletter* (cake in the shape of a letter), one for my mother in the letter *M* (for mother), or at times mother would order one from the bakery in the shape of a *B* (for van den Boom, our family name).

"On Christmas there were no presents. It is a religious day, set aside for church and family gatherings. If Christmas happened to fall on Monday, we went to the two regular church services on Sunday, then twice on Monday (Christmas Day) and again twice on the Second Day of Christmas (Tuesday). That was a lot of church!"

Dutch Speculaas

Crunchy *Speculaas* cookies were traditionally shaped in elaborately carved molds, but are just as delicious cut in squares sprinkled with almonds. In Holland, St. Nicholas rewards good children with *Speculaas*, *Pepernoten* (peppernut cookies), and *Tai Tai* (a gingerbread-like cookie).

½ cup butter or margarine	½ tsp. salt
1 cup brown sugar	1 tsp. cinnamon
1 egg	½ tsp. cloves
2 tbsp. milk	½ tsp. nutmeg
2½ cups flour	⅛ tsp. cardamom
½ tsp. baking powder	½ cup sliced almonds

Cream butter and sugar until fluffy. Add egg and milk. Beat well. Sift together dry ingredients and blend slowly into creamed mixture. Chill overnight.

For Squares or Cookie Cutters: Roll well-chilled dough on floured board. Cut with floured cutter or cut in squares or rectangles with knife. Place on greased baking sheet. Sprinkle with sliced almonds. Bake at 300° for 12-15 minutes or until edges start to brown. Cool on racks. Store in airtight container.

For Molded Cookies: Chill dough in freezer 15 minutes. Generously flour inside of mold. On well-floured board, roll dough thick enough to fill inside of mold. Cut piece of dough to fit in mold and press in. Flatten with floured rolling pin. Slide spatula across to remove excess dough. Remove immediately by turning mold over and tapping on back. Ease cookie onto greased baking sheet.

For large mold, lay greased sheet on mold, invert to release cookie. Bake at 300° about 20 minutes or until edges begin to brown. Cool. Store in airtight container. Makes 1½ dozen.

Ans van den Hoogen, a professional baker, says *Speculaas* retain clearer details of the mold when dough is very stiff and less baking powder is used. Baker van den Hoogen allows, however, "In our shop we go more for flavor and are not so concerned with shape."

Johanna Hekkert, Sunnyvale, California, collects old Speculaas *molds, some of which are two to three feet high, and uses them as wall decorations. She also celebrates St. Nicholas Day with her children by filling their shoes with small gifts and baking large batches of this St. Nicholas Day treat.*

The Famous Honey Cakes of Nürnberg

Long before there was sugar, monks in the monastery kitchens near Nürnberg, Germany, were baking *Lebkuchen* from honey that was brought to them by beekeepers in the nearby Lorenz Forest.

At that time baking powder was unknown, too, so honey became the leavening agent. Mixed with flour, it was left to ferment several months, which gave the dough its lifting power and the famous *Lebkuchen* flavor as well. Fourth-century honey cakes were simply made of flour, honey, and spices.

After Nürnberg was settled, a trade route opened to Venice in the 14th century, making available ginger, cinnamon, nutmeg, anise, almonds, rosewater, citron, and oranges, which were added to the honey cakes. And so *Lebkuchen,* as they are known today, came into being—Nürnberg's first specialty. More than 70 million *Lebkuchen* are baked in that city each year.

Today a number of these simple honey cake bakers still survive in Hungary, kneading honey into flour and pressing the dough into ancient picture molds. A few itinerant bakers shape their cakes into large 12-inch hearts with elaborate icings, pictures, and even tiny mirrors for decoration.

Nürnberger Lebkuchen
(Honey Cookies)

1 cup honey
¾ cup dark brown
  sugar
1 egg, beaten
1 tbsp. lemon juice
1 tsp. grated lemon
  peel
2½ cups flour
1 tsp. cinnamon

½ tsp. cloves
½ tsp. cardamom
⅛ tsp. nutmeg
½ tsp. salt
½ tsp. soda
⅓ cup finely chopped
  candied orange peel
  and citron
½ cup ground almonds

Heat honey in small pan over medium heat only until it begins to bubble. Do not boil. Remove and cool. Stir in brown sugar, egg, lemon juice, and lemon peel until blended; set aside and cool to lukewarm.

In a large bowl stir together flour (unsifted), spices, salt, and soda. Add honey mixture, candied peel, citron, and almonds, stirring until well blended. Dough will be soft. Cover and refrigerate several days.

On a heavily floured board, roll out a small amount of dough to ⅜-inch thickness. Cut dough in rounds with cutter. Grease baking tin and line with parchment, or place cookies on *Back-*

oblaten.° With fingers, round up cookies toward center. Press almond halves into cookies with half a cherry in center. Bake at 375° 10-12 minutes or until set.

Remove immediately and brush with glaze. If baked on parchment, spread glaze over bottom of cookie as soon as top dries. Store in airtight plastic container; age at least 3 weeks or longer. Makes 20 large cookies.

Lebkuchen dough may also be cut in small heart shapes and topped with Chocolate Glaze.

Glaze I: 1 cup powdered sugar, 5 tbsp. water (or rum).

Glaze II: Boil 1 cup sugar and ½ cup water until first indication of a thread (230°). Remove from heat; stir in ¼ cup powdered sugar. Brush hot icing over cookies. Reheat if necessary. You may also flavor glaze with rosewater.

Chocolate Glaze: 8 oz. semi-sweet chocolate melted over warm water.

°*Backoblaten* (bock-o-blotten) are edible baking discs that keep cookies from sticking to pans.

Zimtsterne
(German Cinnamon Stars)

Cinnamon, a favorite spice at Christmas, enhances these chewy almond stars.

2 egg whites	1 tsp. cinnamon
⅛ tsp. salt	2½ cups + 1 tbsp.
1⅓ cups powdered	ground unblanched
sugar, sifted	almonds
½ tsp. lemon juice	

Beat egg whites until stiff. Beat in salt and powdered sugar, 2 tbsp. at a time. The mixture should be stiff and glossy. Beat additionally as necessary so it retains the mark of a knife blade. Set aside ½ cup of whites to coat cookies. Add nuts, cinnamon, and lemon juice. Stir together gently but thoroughly. Mixture should be heavy and fairly solid. Add more almonds if too sticky.

Sprinkle board with sugar and roll dough to ⅜-inch thickness. If dough sticks, sprinkle more sugar on board. Cut dough with small star-shaped cutter. Place on greased baking sheet. Paint each cookie with reserved egg white mixture. Bake at 275° for 20 minutes. Store in airtight container. Makes 2 dozen.

German Kringel

Hard-cooked egg yolks give this cookie a rich, delicate texture. The word *Kringel* means ring or circle.

½ cup butter
½ cup sugar
1 raw egg yolk
3 hard-cooked egg
    yolks, sieved
½ tsp. cardamom
    (optional)

Grated peel of 1
    lemon
2 cups cake flour
1 egg white
Sugar
½ cup finely chopped
    blanched almonds

Beat butter and sugar until creamy. Add raw egg yolk, hard-cooked egg yolks, cardamom, and lemon peel. Mix well. Add sifted cake flour, ½ cup at a time. Mix well. Chill overnight and roll out to ¼-inch thickness on lightly floured board. Cut with 2½-inch doughnut cutter.

Brush tops of *Kringel* with slightly beaten egg white and sprinkle with sugar and almonds. Line baking pan with waxed paper or parchment and set *Kringel* on paper. Bake at 375° for 12 15 minutes or until lightly browned. Cool. Makes about 2 dozen.

Nürnberg's Christmas Market

To visit the Christmas market in Nürnberg, Germany, is to become a child again. Here, in the shadow of the old historic *Frauenkirche*, radiating from a large central créche, are hundreds of little lamplit stalls decked with garlands of evergreen.

Irresistible aromas of sizzling *Bratwurst* served with mustard, horseradish, and German potato salad tempt even the staunchest dieter. Farther on, tantalizing stalls offer burnt sugar almonds, the richest of chocolates, colorful marzipan shaped in a garden array of fruits and vegetables. Nearby, too, is one of the famous *Lebkuchen* bakers with oven-fresh honey cookies for sale.

Mingled with the food is a dazzling array of toys to warm the heart of child and adult alike—beautifully handcrafted dolls, trains, cars, the tiniest of Christmas tree ornaments, brightly painted wooden soldiers, straw stars, wax angels, as well as practical gifts of hand-knit sweaters, mittens, and socks.

There is laughter and music from a children's choir caroling on the steps of the *Frauenkirche*.

An ancient legend has it that once the Christ child, drawn by the glittering lights, children's songs, and the aroma of warm, spicy *Lebkuchen*, came down from heaven to do his Christmas shopping at the fair. Since then it has been called the *Christkindlesmarket* (Christ child's market). Every small Nürnberg child deems it wise to be good in December, since it is the *Christkind* who brings gifts on Christmas Eve—and he just may be at the market anytime, doing his Christmas shopping.

German Spitzbuben
(Little Rogues)

A cookie baker's cookie, *Spitzbuben* are served in many German, Austrian, and Swiss homes at Christmas. Sometimes they are called *Drei Augen* (Three Eyes).

1 cup + 4 tbsp. sweet butter	⅛ tsp. cinnamon
⅔ cup sugar	Strawberry or raspberry jam or currant jelly
2 cups flour	Confectioners' sugar

Beat butter and sugar until creamy. Beat in sifted flour and cinnamon, ½ cup at a time. Shape dough into ball. Wrap in waxed paper and chill overnight.

On lightly floured surface or between waxed or parchment paper, roll dough to ⅛-inch thickness. Cut rounds with 2-inch scalloped cutter. With a plain round cutter, 1 inch smaller, cut a hole in center of *half of the circles* to form top ring.

Another variation of this cookie is to cut out 3 small holes (an inverted pastry tip or screw cap from soft drink bottle works well) in the *top* cookie to form three "eyes."

Place all circles on tins lined with parchment and bake at 350° about 12-15 minutes or until golden brown. Transfer to rack after 1 minute. Dust *top* circles with confectioners' sugar.

Spread about ½ tsp. jelly over each *solid* cookie. Cover with sugared top. Spoon extra dab jelly in opening of each cookie. If storing, fill just before serving. Makes 2 dozen.

There were times during World War II when even a slice of black bread was a luxury in Germany. Consequently, to bake something special for Christmas was nearly impossible. Housewives had to save, beg, or barter for a little extra shortening, flour, or sugar to make even a few cookies or a torte.

Yet, somehow, they did manage to make even those bleak days festive. Magdalena Meyer remembers turning mashed potatoes—with a little almond flavoring and a few nuts—into an ersatz (substitute) marzipan for a Christmas treat.

Springerle

Springerle are among Germany's most famous Christmas cookies. The squares are pressed from wooden molds in countless prints. Helen Epp, a rare person to enjoy the diamond anniversary of marriage and homemaking, shares her favorite *Springerle* recipe from her own cookie collection.

4 eggs	½ tsp. baking ammonia°
2 cups sugar	or ¼ tsp. baking powder
4 drops oil of anise or	Grated peel of ½ lemon
¼ tsp. anise extract	4 cups cake flour
	4 tsp. anise seed

Beat eggs until thick and lemon-colored. Gradually add sugar and beat until mixture is almost white and thick enough to "ribbon." (This makes finished cookie fine grained.) Add anise flavoring, lemon peel, and ammonia dissolved in 1 tsp. water. Gradually add sifted cake flour. Dough should be very firm. Add a little flour if necessary. Chill at least 2 hours.

Dust wooden molds with cornstarch; tap off excess starch. Turn dough onto lightly floured board and roll to ¼-inch thickness. Press dusted wooden molds into dough, bearing down firmly and evenly to leave clear-cut designs. With a floured knife, cut cookies apart. Place on greased baking sheet sprinkled with anise seed. Cover with tea towel and let stand in cool place overnight or up to 24 hours to dry.

In the morning place in 375° oven to set the design; immediately turn down to 300° and bake for 15 minutes. Remove to racks to cool. For softer cookies, let stand overnight before storing in airtight containers. Age 2-3 weeks before serving. (A slice of apple added to the tin the day before serving will soften cookies.) Makes 6 dozen.

°Baking ammonia is available in some European delis.

Some people think the name Springerle *refers to* Springer, *the German name for the knight in a chess game. Others believe it goes back to pagan times when sacrifices were made to the gods. The poor, having no offering, made token gifts in the form of cookies with animal shapes.*

Hints to Springerle Bakers

Springerle bakers suggest that the shape of the cookie varies, depending on the consistency of the dough, whether it is stiff or soft, and what kind of leavening is used. German bakers used *baking ammonia* or *potash*.

Springerle must dry overnight. Then when placed in the oven, only the top of the cookie expands. Because the bottom of the *Springerle* cannot stretch, it stands on "a kind of foot," explains Magdalena Meyer. She suggests sprinkling cookies lightly with water when they come from the oven.

Use cornstarch to dust the mold; it doesn't stick in the fine lines like flour. *Springerle* baking is best done when there is low humidity.

A Christmas Cookie Loft

"Grandmother made all of her Christmas cookies at the end of October," says Magdalena Meyer. *"She tied the cookies in small bags, put them in a pillowcase, and hung them in the attic, high enough, of course, so we grandchildren couldn't reach them. The aging improved the flavor and grandmother's cookies were known to be the most delicious."*

"*To celebrate* Christmas, our Greek homes must be sparkling and spotless," explains Katina Scamagas, San Jose, California. "A lot of attention is given to cleanliness and washing clothes. Mothers bake *Christopsomo*, our Greek Christmas bread, and a lot of *Baklava* and *Melomacarona* (p. 142).

"When I was young, the only Christmas tree in the village was at school. We cut our own pine and decorated it with balloons, little ribbons, and spread cotton around like snow.

"Early Christmas morning—about five o'clock—children go caroling. Some are from the school. They are invited in (village people get up early!) and given sweets and money, which often goes for a school project.

"In Greece it's St. Basil, not Santa Claus, who brings the children gifts. For this occasion he wears a red robe, a red cap, black boots, and carries a large sack, much like the American Santa. Gifts are exchanged on January 1, St. Basil's Day. Christmas in Greece is a religious holiday, a time for church and family."

Greek Kourabiedes

This buttery Greek holiday cookie (pronounced koo-rah-be-*eth*-es) is buried in a blizzard of powdered sugar. It is served at weddings and festivals and especially at Christmas, when a clove is placed in each cookie, a reminder of the spices wise men brought to the Christ child.

1 cup sweet butter	½ tsp. almond extract
⅓ cup powdered sugar	2 cups + 2 tbsp. flour
2 egg yolks	½ cup ground almonds, lightly toasted

Cream butter and sugar. Add egg yolks and flavoring and beat well. Gradually add flour and mix. Add almonds. Form into a ball and chill for 1 hour. Shape dough into 1-inch balls or crescents. Place on greased baking sheet. Make slight indentation on top of each round cookie. Bake at 350° 15-20 minutes or until very lightly browned.

Remove from sheet and place warm cookies in shallow pan. Sift powdered sugar over tops generously. (Cookies must have plenty of sugar on top.) Store in airtight container. Makes about 2½ dozen.

Greek Melomacarona
(Honey Dainties)

These tender cookies are glazed with honey and dipped in nuts. Aristea Pettis, San Jose, California, makes these tempting delights every Christmas.

½ cup butter or margarine	1 egg yolk
1 cup safflower oil	½ tsp. cinnamon
½ cup sugar	⅛ tsp. cloves
½ tsp. grated orange peel	1 tsp. baking powder
½ tsp. grated lemon peel	3½ cups flour
	½ cup orange juice
	Honey Syrup
	Sugar/Nut Topping

Beat margarine or butter, oil, and sugar until creamy. Add lemon and orange peel, and egg yolk. (Here Mrs. Pettis adds 1½ tsp. cognac.) Add flour sifted with baking powder, cinnamon, and cloves alternately with orange juice. Mix well. Cover and chill overnight. With about 1 tbsp. dough, form slightly rounded ovals, 2 x 1½ inches.

Place on greased baking sheet and bake at 325° for 25-30 minutes. Cool. Dip in Honey Syrup and sprinkle with Sugar/

Nut Topping. If storing cookies, wait until serving time to glaze.

Honey Syrup: 1 cup sugar, ½ cup water, ½ cup honey, ½ tsp. lemon juice. Bring all ingredients to a boil and boil gently for 5 minutes. Skim off foam. Place cookies on wire rack over waxed paper. Dip cooled cookies in Honey Syrup (keep it warm). Sprinkle with topping mixture.

Sugar/Nut Topping: Mix together ½ cup sugar, 1 cup ground or finely chopped walnuts, and ¼ tsp. cinnamon. Makes 4 dozen.

"Greek families don't give gifts at Christmas. It is a religious day," says Aristea Pettis. *"We always had a crèche in the corner of the living room. Some of the animals father carved by hand; others we children stuffed and sewed.... There was always caroling the whole week before Christmas, and the baking of* Kourabiedes *and other cookies as well as* Christopsomo, *a round Christmas bread decorated with a large cross and walnuts."*

EVERY ITALIAN family has a Christmas *Presepe*—a manger scene—which is often quite elaborate. Mother brought ours out on the first day of *Novena,* nine days before Christmas. Many of the figures were family heirlooms, handed down for generations.

Each year we added something new—a bit of moss, some stones, another figure. Not only did we have the holy family, shepherds, and wise men, but also familiar village people—an old peasant woman bringing a basket of eggs to the Baby Jesus, a farmer with a head of cabbage, a man with a bundle of faggots to keep the *Bambino* warm. Each morning we lit candles and offered prayers at the *Presepe.* Again on Christmas Eve, when the candles were burning, we said our prayers and mother put the tiny *Bambino* in his crib.

Sometimes itinerant pipers—*Xampognari*—coming down from the mountains, go from house to house and play their pastoral carols in front of the *Presepe.* It is a lovely, moving time. St. Francis of Assisi originated the *Presepe* 700 years ago. (*Matilde Oliverio shared holiday customs from her childhood in Naples, Italy, with her Italian language students in San Jose, California.*)

Italian Biscotti

These twice-baked cookies make great coffee dunkers.

3 eggs
1 cup sugar
¾ cup vegetable oil
2 tsp. anise seed
   or 1 tsp. vanilla

3 cups flour
2 tsp. soda
½ tsp. salt
1 cup chopped almonds
   or walnuts

Beat eggs until thick and lemon-colored. Gradually add sugar and beat; add oil. Lightly crush anise seed with mortar and pestle. Add to egg mixture. Sift flour, salt, and soda together and gradually add to egg mixture. Beat until smooth. Add nuts. Turn out onto lightly floured board and shape into flat loaves about ½-inch thick and 2½ inches wide, the length of the baking sheet. Place on greased baking sheets. Bake at 375° for 20 minutes.

Remove from oven; cool 2 minutes and slice into ¾-inch pieces. Lay slices, cut side down, on baking sheets. Bake again at 375° for 10 minutes or until just golden brown. Remove to wire racks and cool. *Biscotti* keep very well in airtight containers. Makes about 4 dozen.

Pizzelle

A holiday favorite in Italian homes, *Pizzelle* are baked in a decorative iron on top of the stove. Lonnie De Vincenzi and several friends bake more than a thousand dozen (!) *Pizzelle* for the Italian-American Heritage Festival in San Jose, California. Loni and her husband co-chair this festal occasion.

2 eggs	1 tsp. crushed anise
6 tbsp. sugar	seed or 3 drops oil
¼ cup melted butter	of anise
½ tsp. vanilla	1 cup flour

Beat eggs until light. Beat in sugar, cooled melted butter, vanilla, and anise seed. Stir in flour. Heat *Pizzelle* iron until hot. Brush lightly with butter. Add a spoonful of batter and bake 1 minute. Turn iron over and bake until both sides are golden. Using a spatula, transfer cookie to wire rack. Makes 14.

Jeannie Snyder's Cuccidati
(Italian Fig Cookies)

This popular combination of dried fruits, nuts, and pastry came to this country from Sicily. Baked in long rolls and sliced, or tucked into pastry pockets, *Cuccidati* (koo-chi-*da*-ti) are made in many Italian homes and bakeries at Christmas. The recipe comes from Jeannie Bertucelli Snyder, food editor of the Italian/American Heritage paper, in San Jose, California.

Filling

¾ cup each dried figs, prunes, raisins

⅓ cup dates

1 cup glazed fruit cake mix

¾ cup each toasted ground almonds and walnuts

¼ cup chocolate chips (optional)

½ cup water

¼ cup apple juice°

½ cup sugar

¼ tsp. cinnamon

1½ tsp. vanilla

Grind all fruit, fruit cake mix, and nuts into a large bowl. Add chocolate chips (optional), but do *not* grind. In a saucepan, bring to a boil water, sugar, apple juice.

°Traditionally, 2 tbsp. EACH of rum and brandy are used for flavoring *in place of apple juice* and are added *after* the sugar syrup.

Add sugar syrup to fruit mixture and let stand overnight. If mixture is dry, add a little more syrup or hot water.

Pastry

2 cups flour	½ cup shortening
2 tsp. baking powder	1 tsp. vanilla
¼ tsp. salt	1 egg, beaten
	4½ tbsp. milk

Sift dry ingredients together and cut in shortening as for pie dough. Combine egg, vanilla, and milk; add to flour and mix lightly into a ball. Divide in half. Roll half of dough into 4 x 18-inch rectangle. Place filling mixture down center of strip. Wet edges of dough with milk. Fold over and seal edges and ends. Make a few slits on top to allow steam to escape. Repeat with remaining pastry and filling. (Thickness of dough should resemble commercial fig newtons.) Please turn page.

Place loaves on greased baking sheet, seam side down. Bake at 325° 25-30 minutes or until golden brown. When cool, slice in 3-inch pieces (or smaller). Glaze each piece with mixture of 1 cup confectioners' sugar and 1½ tbsp. water or milk. Sprinkle with *nonpareil* decorating candies.

Steffani ("Stella") Silva's family has been making Cuccidati *from the same Sicilian recipe for more than a hundred years. "Grandmother made her fruit squares rather large, decorating them with designs of pastry dough—pyrocantha wreaths, birds in a nest, Christmas trees, or fish, cutting tiny scales with a scissors. Because* Cuccidati *are rich, I prefer to make my squares smaller—just bite size," she says.*

Mrs. Silva's grandmother added orange to her recipe. Baking the orange before grinding gave the filling a lovely, unique flavor.

150

Steffani Silva's Cuccidati

(Italian Fig Cookies)

Filling

⅔ cup dried apricots
1 cup or 8 oz. dates
1½ cups raisins
1 12-oz. pkg dried
    white figs
1 cup glazed fruit cake
    mix
½ large orange

1 cup chopped nuts
1 cup honey
½ tsp. each nutmeg,
    cinnamon, cloves,
    black pepper (optional)
    and vanilla
½ tsp. rum extract
    (optional)

Dice apricots and fruit cake mix; set aside. Grind dried fruits and orange with rind into large bowl. Add apricots, fruit cake mix, nuts, honey, spices, and flavorings. Mix well. Soften filling with hot water; add sugar only to taste. Let stand overnight.

To finish *Cuccidati,* follow pastry, glazing, and decorating directions, pp. 149 and 150. Double pastry recipe. Makes 4 18-inch loaves. Slice in 1-inch pieces or larger.

IN THE SMALL Italian village where Angela Gagliardi grew up, St. Barbara's Day has special meaning. Barbara not only is the patron saint of Piane Crati, but the village church bears her name as well.

Each year on December 4, the women of Piane Crati celebrate *Pitanza* with a feast table laden with breads and pastries in honor of their saint, who as a young girl, disobeyed her father's wishes and shared grain with the poor. Village people go from house to house saying, "*Pitanza!*" meaning "Give me a pittance." No one is refused on this day.

Ever since Mrs. Gagliardi came to this country she has kept this village tradition with an open house on St. Barbara's Day. At 82, she still bakes a wide array of her native Calabrian delicacies and invites more than 100 friends to her special *Pitanza* in her San Jose, California, home. No one is turned away. Before leaving, each guest is given a tiny replica of St. Barbara's hands which Mrs. Gagliardi fashions out of *Tarali* dough.

One year Angela was hospitalized on the feast day. This posed a real problem: Never had she broken her tradition! But thanks to family and friends who brought a *portable Pitanza*, Angela kept the custom—even in her hospital room. And no one was turned away.

Angela Gagliardi vows that as long as she is able, her home will be open to celebrate the Feast of *Pitanza* every December 4.

MEXICO contributes many colorful traditions to the Christmas celebration, but perhaps the most loved by children is the breaking of the *Piñata* on Christmas Eve.

Bought at the marketplace or made at home, *Piñatas* are big earthenware jars decorated with cardboard and brightly colored tissue paper in the shapes of animals, flowers, or huge paper stars.

Oranges, bananas, tangerines, peanuts, and pieces of sugarcane are stuffed into the jar which is suspended from a rope so it may be pulled up and down. Each child is blindfolded, given a stick, spun in a circle, and told to swing at the *Piñata*. If he swishes the air near the guests, everyone shrieks with fear and laughter. When at last someone cracks the jar, the children scramble to pick up their treats. Extra baskets of tropical fruits are shared by the hostess with the rest of her guests.

Originating in Italy, the *Piñata* tradition came to Spain where it took on religious significance during the Lenten season. In Mexico it is part of the Christmas *Posada* celebration.

THE BIGGEST event in our village in Mexico was the Christmas *Posada* (meaning inn), remembers Rosa Calvillo, Milpitas, California. When I was a little girl, everyone in the parish was invited. For nine evenings we went to nine different homes. Two children, carrying images of Mary and Joseph, led the candlelight procession around the house, singing traditional songs and asking for shelter. Each time the innkeeper replied, "No room!"

After being turned away several times, we were finally welcomed at the last door on which they knocked. The procession entered the house and we placed our lighted candles around the *Nacimiento* (crèche). After the religious ceremony, there was a *Piñata* for the children. On Christmas Eve we celebrated with *Tamales*, *Buñuelos*, hot chocolate, and candy-covered almonds.

"The next morning we got up early and went to sunrise mass. It was a big thrill to see the beautiful nativity scene where the Baby Jesus had been laid. We lined up to go by the crèche to make sure he was there!"

154

155

Mexican Buñuelos
(Fried Sweet Fritters)

Crisp, fluffy rounds, sprinkled with cinnamon and sugar, make a perfect complement to mugs of frothy hot chocolate on Christmas Eve. *Buñuelos* (boo-ny*ue*-los) are traditional among Mexican people, wherever they live.

4 eggs	1 tsp. baking powder
¼ cup sugar	1 tsp. salt
1 tsp. vegetable oil	1 cup sugar
2 cups flour	1 tsp. cinnamon

In a bowl, combine eggs and sugar and beat until thick and lemon-colored. Add oil. Combine 1½ cups unsifted flour, baking powder, and salt, and gradually add to eggs. Beat well. Turn dough onto board, using remaining flour. Knead until smooth and elastic.

Shape dough into 16 balls. Roll each ball into a 5-inch circle. Lay on waxed paper, uncovered, about 10 minutes. Fry in deep hot oil at 350° until golden brown, turning once. Drain on paper towels. Sprinkle with cinnamon/sugar mixture. Store in airtight container.

There is much laughter and good fun while making Buñuelos *in Rosa Calvillo's home on Christmas Eve. Rosa "calls out the troops" and rounds up everyone—uncles, aunts, grandmothers, children—to help roll out their* Buñuelos *(p. 156). "Everyone works, even if it means rolling the dough on a cloth on your lap. I like it because it brings my whole family together," she says.*

Good food and good Buñuelos *are traditions Rosa adopted from her grandmother, Aurora Larriva, a fine cook who sold* Tacos, Burritos, *and* Tortas *from a small sidewalk vending stand in the little Mexican village of Torreon (Coahuila). "Grandmother was always making something special. That's where I learned to cook."*

Biscochitos

"*Biscochitos* are Spanish," explains Lodean Phillips, who makes them in her Los Alamos, New Mexico, home. "They are traditional at Christmas and are used for weddings and feast days. I've also eaten them on feast days of Indian friends in their pueblo homes.... *Biscochitos* are crisp and lightly flavored with anise—a cookie that is very easy to eat."

½ cup sugar
1 cup lard
1 egg, beaten
½ tsp. anise extract
1½ tsp. crushed anise
   seed

1½ tsp. baking powder
½ tsp. salt
3½ tbsp. orange juice
3½ cups flour
Cinnamon-sugar
   topping

Cream lard. Add sugar, egg, extract, anise seed; beat well. Sift baking powder, flour, and salt. Add gradually to first mixture. Add orange juice and blend. Chill overnight. Roll ⅛-inch thick and cut into shapes. Dip top of each cookie in mixture of ¼ cup sugar and ½ tsp. cinnamon. Place on greased baking sheet. Bake at 375° for 5-7 minutes or just until edges turn golden brown. Watch closely. Cool.

IN POLISH farm homes sheaves of grain, brought into the house on Christmas Eve, are tied with colored ribbons and placed in corners of the room. Prayers are said for a bountiful harvest. Grain, a good crop, and harvest all intertwine with the Christmas festival.

Polish women, even now, put fresh clean straw under the Christmas tablecloth, a reminder of the manger in Bethlehem.

"In Serbian homes they used to scatter straw around the whole house," relates Dusanka Tkachenko, "but now in America, it's mainly done in the churches (Serbian)."

She recalled, too, the earlier yule log ceremony when the mother threw a handful of wheat over the log as it was brought in. The father announced, "Christ is born!" And the family replied, "Indeed, he is born!"

Sometimes the whole family formed a procession behind the mother, going from room to room, covering floors with straw. In the kitchen they gathered around a box of wheat with a tall lighted candle while the father prayed for health, happiness, and good crops in the coming year. After this came the Christmas Eve supper.

Polish Poppy Seed Cookies

Poppy seeds are a favorite in Polish Christmas baking. Here is a simple combination of a delicate butter cookie and a crunchy poppy seed topping.

1 cup butter	2 raw egg yolks
¾ cup sugar	2 cups flour
1 tsp. vanilla	½ tsp. salt
2 hard-cooked egg yolks, sieved	Egg White Glaze
	Poppy seeds

Beat butter, sugar, and vanilla until creamy. Add sieved egg yolks and raw egg yolks to sugar and mix well. Add sifted flour and salt gradually. Chill dough. Roll out small portions to ¼-inch thickness on floured board. Cut in 1½-2-inch rounds. Place on greased baking sheet. Brush with 1 egg white beaten with 1 tbsp. water. Sprinkle with poppy seeds. Bake at 350° for 10-12 minutes or until delicately browned. Makes about 3 dozen.

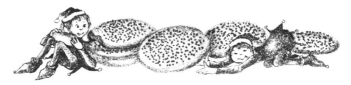

Rumanian Pine Nut Macaroons

Toasted pine nuts accent these airy almond-filled macaroons.

2 egg whites
⅛ tsp. cream of tartar
⅔ cup powdered sugar
⅓ cup sugar
¼ tsp. almond extract

1½ cups ground toasted
  almonds
1¼ oz. pine nuts, slightly
  toasted
¼ cup sugar

Beat egg whites with cream of tartar until foamy. Add sugar gradually; add almond extract and beat until very stiff. Gently fold in almonds. Cover cookie sheet with parchment. Drop meringue mixture by teaspoonfuls over a few pine nuts. Sprinkle tops of meringues with remaining pine nuts and granulated sugar.

Bake at 350° for 15 minutes or until golden brown. Cool and store in airtight container. Makes 3 dozen.

Danish Christmas Eve Supper

RISENGRÖD (Rice Porridge)

GAASESTEG MED AEBLER OG SVESKER
(Roast Goose with Apples and Prunes)

RØDKAAL (Red Cabbage)

BRUNEDE KARTOFLER (Browned Potatoes)

KAFFEE (Coffee)

AEBLEKAGE, JULEKAGE
(Apple Cake, Christmas Cake)

LIKÖRER (Liqueurs)

THERE IS AN old saying in Denmark that the spirit of Christmas must not leave the house. Danish housewives capture the spirit by offering Christmas baking to everyone who comes to the door.

Early in December they bake hundreds of cookies. Family recipes may yield ten dozen or more and it is not unusual for some women to turn out 300 *Brune Kager* (brown cakes). Cookie batters are stirred early so flavors and spices mingle before baking.

A final test of good Danish cookies is crispness. Butter helps, and so does careful rolling, they say. But there is still another ingredient in Scandinavian recipes that makes their cookies lighter and thinner—*salt of hartshorn,* or baking ammonia *(ammonium bicarbonate).* For instance, in Karen Berg's little book, *Danish Home Baking,* most of the cookie recipes call for *salt of hartshorn.*

Baking ammonia predates baking powder and once was made from the antlers of a deer. Now it is produced chemically. The aroma is potent, but when baked, there is not a trace. Results are worth the slight discomfort. Baking ammonia is available in many European delicatessens.

Finskbröd
(Finnish Shortbread)

Baked in Denmark and throughout Scandinavia, Finnish shortbread is a popular light, buttery cookie made for the Christmas holiday.

1 cup sifted flour	1 egg white
¼ cup sugar	¼ cup finely chopped
½ cup ground almonds	almonds
½ cup butter	2 tbsp. sugar

In a mixing bowl, combine flour, sugar, and ground almonds. Cut in butter and mix into a soft dough. Wrap and chill 15 minutes. Roll dough into ½-inch ropes, laying ropes parallel to each other. With a sharp knife, cut across in 2-inch pieces. Brush with beaten egg white. Dip each piece in a mixture of chopped almonds and sugar.

Place cookies slightly apart on greased baking sheet. Bake at 350° about 15 minutes or until golden brown. Cool on cookie sheet and remove carefully. Makes about 4½ dozen.

Berliner Kranser
(Berlin Wreaths)

Liz Nelson, Los Gatos, California, offers this Norwegian favorite on her holiday cookie trays. "I decorate my wreaths with bits of red and green cherries, but my (Norwegian) mother doesn't think that's right at all!"

1 cup butter	¼ tsp. each lemon and
½ cup sugar	orange extract
2 raw egg yolks	½ tsp. vanilla°
2 hard-cooked egg	2½ cups flour
yolks, sieved	

Beat butter and sugar until creamy. Stir in raw and hard-cooked egg yolks and flavoring. Add flour and mix until smoothly blended. Chill briefly. Cut off small amounts of dough and roll in pencil-thin strips. Form a circle and loop one end over and through. Brush wreaths with 1 egg beaten with 1 tbsp. water and dip in coarse (crushed loaf) sugar.

Place on greased baking sheet and bake at 350° for 12-15 minutes or until golden brown. Remove immediately. Makes 5 dozen.

°Alternate flavoring: ½ tsp. almond extract *only*. Top wreath with mixture of sugar and ground almonds.

"My mother always made *Fattigman* for Christmas. She stored them in airtight containers in the coolest place in the house—on the steps leading to the attic, which was quite cold in our Minnesota home," says Muriel Schlichting of San Jose, California. "*Fattigman* stay fresh a long time that way."

° ° °

"My mother, who is now 84, still bakes *Klenor* (the Swedish version of *Fattigman*) every Christmas, but not in such big quantities as before," writes Dr. Ingrid Gamstorp of Uppsala. "*Klenor* are often served with berries, preferably raspberries and whipped cream, as a dessert, perhaps together with a glass of port wine."

° ° °

Fattigmans Bakkels, Norwegian crullers dusted with powdered sugar, are known in Sweden as *Klenor*, in Denmark as *Klenje*, and the Finns call them *Klenetit*, all meaning small or little.

Fattigmans Bakkels

In Norwegian, *Fattigmans Bakkels* means poor man's baked goods. Not anymore! But they are well worth the price and effort.

4 egg yolks	¼ cup whipping cream
⅓ cup sugar	½ tsp. cardamom
½ tsp. grated lemon peel	1½ cups flour

Beat egg yolks, sugar, and lemon peel until very thick. (Traditionally, 1 tbsp. brandy is added to the mixture to cut the grease.) Add cream slowly, mixing well. Sift flour and cardamom; add gradually to eggs. Wrap dough and chill overnight. Heat oil (Scandinavian bakers insist lard gives *Fattigman* a better flavor) to 365° or 370°.

Roll dough 1/16-inch thick on floured surface or between sheets of waxed paper. With a pastry wheel cut in diamond shapes, 3 x 2 inches wide. Make lengthwise slit down center of each and tuck under and pull through. Handle dough lightly. Fry to golden brown; turn. Drain on paper towels. Cool. Sprinkle with confectioners' sugar. Store in airtight containers.

Norwegian Sandbakkelser

Liz Nelson grew up in a Norwegian-American home, studies Norwegian, and is active in Sons of Norway. "Norwegians usually serve these tart shells plain, like a cookie," says Liz. Her shells are especially light and flaky.

In Sweden they add ground almonds to the dough and call the tarts *Mandelmusslor*. Both Danes and Swedes may fill the shells with frozen raspberries and whipped cream, raspberry jam, or even a buttercream.

1 cup butter	½ tsp. cardamom
1 cup lard	½ tsp. vanilla
1½ cups sugar	¼ tsp. almond extract
2 eggs	4 cups flour

Beat butter, lard, and sugar until creamy. Add eggs, one at a time, beating well. Add cardamom, vanilla, and almond. Gradually add sifted flour and knead well. Chill overnight. Press walnut-sized pieces of dough evenly around bottom and sides of *Sandbakkelse* tins.

Bake shells on ungreased baking sheet at 350° for 8-10 minutes. Cool completely in tins. Turn over and tap gently to release. Makes 4 dozen.

STRICTLY FOR the birds! Before sitting down to Christmas dinner, the farmers in Scandinavian countries give the birds their Yuletide feast. The finest sheaf of oats or wheat, saved from the summer's harvest, is put on a pole on top of the barn. This custom is followed in many Scandinavian-American communities.

Ester Harvest, a Danish-American, emphasizes, "It wouldn't be Christmas unless the birds are taken care of!"

Ruth Yoder's Perfect Krumkake

Baked on traditional irons engraved with Christmas or decorative scenes, these crisp cookies, rolled into cone shapes, may be eaten plain or filled with whipped cream and fruit.

Ruth's family recipe comes from her grandmother, Ingaborg Hjertass, who lived in Oslo. "Every Norwegian to whom I've given this recipe likes it and uses it," says Ruth.

1½ cups flour	4 eggs
½ cup cornstarch	1 tsp. fresh ground
¾ cup melted butter	cardamom
1¼ cups sugar	1 cup whipping cream

Sift flour and cornstarch together; set aside. Melt butter over double boiler. Add sugar to butter. Cool. With spatula or wooden spoon, beat in eggs, 1 at a time. Add cardamom.

Beginning with ⅓ cup cream, alternate flour and cream in small amounts, using downward motion to "pull in the flour." Slowly warm seasoned 5-6-inch *Krumkake* iron over medium heat (about 10-15 minutes). Brush with melted butter.

For each cookie spoon about 1 iced teaspoon batter into center of iron; close. Bake over gas flame or electric burner about 20 seconds first side; 30 seconds second side. (Timing depends on your stove.)

Remove hot cookie, leave flat, shape into a cone, or roll into a cylinder with wooden *Krumkake* form (available in kitchenware shops) or inside a glass. Cool on seam on rack. Serve plain or filled with whipped cream and fruit. Makes 75.

Swedish Pepparkakor

Pepparkakor are made in every Swedish home at Christmas. Earlier ginger and pepper were used interchangeably; therefore the pepper prefix for this ginger-flavored cookie.

The original recipe for this cookie, using only ginger as the flavoring, was brought from Sweden by Edith Carlson to her new home in Lindsborg, Kansas, many years ago. It was used to make the *Pepparkakor* for Lindsborg's first *Hyllningsfest* (pioneer festival) in 1941.

½ cup sugar	¼ tsp. cloves
½ cup light molasses	1 tbsp. grated orange peel
½ cup butter	1½ tsp. soda
1 tsp. ginger	1 egg, beaten
½ tsp. cinnamon	2 cups flour
½ tsp. mace or nutmeg	¼ tsp. salt

Combine first 8 ingredients in a saucepan over low heat; bring to a boil, remove from heat and stir in soda. Cool to lukewarm and add egg. Gradually mix in sifted flour and salt. (Dough is quite soft.) Chill overnight. Roll out 1/16-inch thick, using as little flour as possible on pastry board. Cut in shapes of hearts, stars, roosters, reindeer.

Place on greased baking sheet and bake at 375° for 5-7 minutes or until cookies are golden brown. Cool on pans. Outline edges of cookies with Royal Icing. Makes 7 dozen 2-inch cookies.

Royal Icing: Beat at high speed 1 egg white with ⅛ tsp. cream of tartar and dash of salt for 1 minute. Add 2 cups sifted powdered sugar. Beat slowly until blended. At high speed beat until very stiff (3-5 minutes). Press through decorating tube with plain tip. Allow frosting to dry before storing.

A Swedish Pepparkakor *tree is topped with a sheaf of wheat. The wooden rods are tipped with bright red apples and frosted* Pepparkakor *are hung from the wooden branches.*

AFTER ST. LUCIA'S DAY (December 13) cookie baking begins in earnest in Scandinavian homes.

In earlier times, housewives used to get up as early as 4:00 in the morning, tiptoe down to their cold kitchens, and begin mixing their Christmas cookies. An old superstition had it that no sunlight should shine on the dough or disaster would befall the household. Every housewife hoped for a crescent moon lingering on the horizon to bring good luck to her baking.

Housewives still love to outdo each other, making hundreds and hundreds of cookies of many varieties. Formerly they were packed in tightly covered tins until the afternoon of the 24th when, according to tradition, folks were allowed to taste them for the first time.

Before going to church on Christmas, mothers frequently set out piles of goodies for each member of the family. And children ate to their heart's content when they returned home after the service.

Christmas baking is enjoyed especially after Christmas Day when there is more time to sit and chat, sip coffee, and eat the Christmas cookies and cakes.

Swedish Spritz

A Christmas favorite in Scandinavia, these buttery *Spritz* are a wonderful time saver in a busy season.

1 cup butter	1 tsp. almond extract
⅔ cup sugar	⅓ tsp. cream of tartar
3 egg yolks	⅛ tsp. salt
	2½ cups flour

Beat butter and sugar together until creamy. Add egg yolks and almond extract and mix well. Sift together flour, cream of tartar, and salt. Gradually add to creamed mixture, mixing until smooth. Pack dough into a cookie tube press and shape dough in circles or S's on greased baking sheet.

Using the thin, flat wafer cutout, press long strips of dough onto greased baking sheets. Bake at 350° for 8-10 minutes or until edges of cookies are golden brown. With sharp knife, cut diagonally across strips, making 2½-inch cookies. Remove and cool on racks. Makes 5 dozen wafers or 40-50 shaped cookies.

TALES OF TROLLS and goblins have long been part of Nordic lore, passed on by grandmothers from one generation to the next. In Denmark, the *Julnisse* (Christmas elves) are said to live in every barn, protecting house and animals from harm. The Swedes' lovable *Tomte* is a cross between an Irish leprechaun and the Dutch St. Nicholas. A pointed cap and flowing white beard identify the *Julnisse* of Norway.

If not treated properly, the story goes, these little pranksters will mix up milk buckets, tangle horses' manes, and even make cows sick. So it is traditional at Christmas for the Scandinavians to reward their *Nisse* with a bowlful of rice for his faithful protection.

Thyra Bjorn writes, "Even as we outgrew many of these superstitions, it was still hard to realize that our beloved *Tomte* was a myth and that he did not really eat the big bowlful of rice porridge we set on the step on Christmas Eve."°

Today this tradition is kept mainly by grandparents for the sake of their children.

°Thyra Ferre Bjorn, *Once upon a Christmas Time* (New York, N.Y.: Holt, Rinehart, Winston).

A Scotch Hogmanay Supper

(New Year's Eve)

KIPPER CREAM
(Kippered Herring in Cream Sauce)

AYRSHIRE BACON OR HAM

SALADS

BLACK BUN
(Fruit/Nut Filling in a Pastry Shell)

SHORTBREAD

Scotch Shortbread

In Scotland, shortbread is traditionally made only for New Year's Eve. Doreen Leith, a native of Glasgow, makes hers in a 6-inch circle. When it comes from the oven, she sprinkles it with sugar and quickly scores it into 16 wedges. When cool, it is broken, rather than cut, for good luck.

Doreen's mother says, "Good shortbread requires cold butter and cold hands so the oil won't run in the butter." The dough may be soft, but not sticky.

½ cup sweet butter	1 cup flour
¼ cup superfine sugar	½ cup rice flour°

Cream butter and sugar. Sift flours together. Work into butter mixture until smooth; form into a ball. Chill. Pat dough into 6 or 7-inch circle. Flute edges. Place on pan lined with waxed paper. Bake at 325° for 40-45 minutes or until golden brown and done in the center.

Using a knife, score into 16 triangles; sprinkle lightly with sugar while hot. Cool on rack. Break into pieces for serving. Makes 1 shortbread.

°Available in health food stores.

Lang May Yur Lum Reek!

The celebration of *Hogmanay*, or New Year, belongs most truly to the Scots.

Though the origin of the word is lost, the custom derives from the good fairy of Norse folklore. At midnight the menfolk set out to "first-foot" neighbors and friends—the first man to cross the threshold of a home in the New Year is the first-foot.

Traditionally, a first-foot brings with him a piece of coal, a bottle of Scotch, and a piece of bread or a thin oat cake. The lump of coal is shared with the rousing wish, "Lang may yur lum reek!" (Long may your chimney smoke!) "A wee dram of Scotch" is said to bring the friend good luck, and bread expresses the hope they may be well provided for.

Doreen Leith's father, Ernest LeSage, had first-footed a dear friend for more than 40 years. When the Leith's second child was born, Doreen's father delayed a visit to see his new grandson because it was *Hogmanay*. His friend, who was ill, had requested that Mr. LeSage first-foot him, as he had for so long. It was important to her father to remain in Glasgow to carry on this tradition—and welcome his new grandson later.

"In our home we first-foot, too," Doreen relates. "We always have a big *Hogmanay* party, and at midnight, my husband,

David, goes outside and knocks. I answer the door. He wishes everyone a good New Year—sometimes he brings with him chocolates or bread.... A first-footer should be tall, dark, and handsome, for good luck, and David fits all three."

First-footing is carried on into January. It also has significance for the first time you visit someone's home. "My mother always took a gift, a plant, some heather, or some small thing whenever she made a first visit to another home." (*Doreen Leith is a teacher and lives in Palo Alto, California.*)

Basler Leckerli

¾ cup good quality
honey
1 cup sugar
3 tbsp. lemon juice°
2 cups finely chopped
almonds
⅔ cup chopped candied
orange and lemon peel

Grated peel of ½ lemon
4 tsp. cinnamon
1 tsp. nutmeg
½ tsp. cloves
1 tsp. baking powder
3 cups flour
Leckerli Glaze

Melt honey in a large saucepan (not over 122° F); do not boil. Remove from heat. Add sugar and lemon juice and stir until dissolved. Cool to lukewarm. Gradually add ¾ of the flour sifted with spices and baking powder. Mix well. Add remaining ingredients. Turn out onto board with remaining flour and knead it into the dough. Dough will be stiff. Cover tightly and chill for several days.

Bring dough to room temperature. On floured board, roll dough to fit 10 x 14-inch tin. Place in greased and floured baking pan. Bake at 350° for about 30 minutes or until done. Brush

---

°Most Swiss recipes use Kirsch in place of lemon juice for tenderness. If using Kirsch, omit baking powder.

off excess flour. Brush with glaze while still hot. Cool and cut into 2 x 3-inch rectangles. Store in airtight container several weeks before serving.

Leckerli Glaze: 1 cup powdered sugar mixed with 3 tbsp. lemon juice.

𝕭𝖆𝖘𝖑𝖊𝖗 𝕷𝖊𝖈𝖐𝖊𝖗𝖑𝖎

Basel, the old Swiss city along the Rhine, boasts this specialty which goes back 500 years. With minor exceptions, these spicy honey cookies remain much the same today as those made by the proud Basel burghers back in the fifteenth century.

During the Christmas season, these famous confections are baked in every home and sold in markets and bakeries all over Switzerland. Irvine Nussbaumer, who manages Migros bakeries in Basel and Tesin, says they bake from three to four tons of *Leckerli* every week during Christmas. Mr. Nussbaumer notes that the quality of honey used is important—get the best, and one low in sugar content.

My introduction to *Leckerli* (meaning delicious) was in the home of Erna Würgler many Christmases ago in Basel. Erna's recipe (page 182) comes from her baker husband, Jacques. *Leckerli,* like good friendships, improve with age.

183

Sablés

Topped with tangy lemon glaze, *Sablés* (meaning sand or dry cake) are the ultimate in delectable butter cookies. This delicacy is part of the baking repertoire of Lilly Gyger, who bakes Swiss cakes and tortes for a homey little restaurant at Bienenberg, overlooking the village of Liestal, Switzerland.

½ cup + 3½ tbsp. sweet butter
⅓ cup + 1½ tsp. sugar
½ tsp. salt

1 tsp. vanilla
　or ½ pkg. vanilla sugar
2 cups flour
Lemon Glaze

Cream butter. Add sugar and beat until creamy. Add vanilla and salt. Add sifted flour gradually. Mix well. Shape into a 2-inch round roll. Wrap in plastic or waxed paper. Chill overnight. Cut in thin slices. Bake on greased baking sheet. Bake at 350° for 8-10 minutes or until golden brown around the edges. Remove from pan. Glaze while hot. Makes about 3 dozen.

Lemon Glaze: Mix together ½ cup powdered sugar and 3 tsp. lemon juice.

Basler Brunsli

Another unique specialty of good bakers in Switzerland is this chocolate-almond, macaroon-meringue cookie. Liesel Widmer, a staff member of the Mennonite Bible school in Liestal, Switzerland, shared this recipe.

4 egg whites
1 cup powdered sugar
1 cup granulated sugar
1 cup ground almonds
1 cup ground filberts

1 tsp. cinnamon
½ tsp. cloves
3 oz. unsweetened baking
  chocolate, ground

In a large mixing bowl, combine ground nuts and chocolate. Set aside. Beat egg whites until foamy. Gradually beat in sugar. Add cinnamon and cloves. Beat until mixture is stiff. Gently fold egg whites into almond-chocolate mixture.

Spread about ⅓ cup sugar on a large board. Sprinkle 2 tbsp. sugar on the top. Roll dough to ¼-inch thickness. Use additional sugar if necessary.

Cut with small shaped cutters or slice into 1 x 2-inch bars. Place on foil or parchment-lined cookie sheet. Bake at 325° for about 15-20 minutes or until dry. Do not overbake. Makes about 4 dozen small cookies.

Hanni Roth's Mandelmailänderli
(Little almond cookies from Milan)

1 cup + 2 tbsp. butter
½ cup sugar
2 eggs
Grated rind of
    ½ lemon

1¼ cups ground
    unblanched almonds
2 cups flour
Egg Glaze

Beat butter and sugar until light and creamy. Add eggs, beating well. Add lemon rind and almonds. Gradually add sifted flour, blending well. Chill dough overnight. On floured surface or between sheets of waxed paper, roll small amounts of dough to ⅛-inch thickness. Keep dough chilled. Cut designs with floured cutter. (Swiss women use *Mailänderli* cutters, 1¼-inch in diameter in shapes of hearts, stars, crescents.)

Place cookies on greased baking sheet. Brush cookies with glaze of 1 egg yolk beaten with 1 tbsp. water. Sprinkle with granulated sugar. Bake at 350° for 10-12 minutes or until golden brown around the edges. Cool on racks.

From late November on, Hanni Roth's Basel kitchen is filled with the marvelous aromas of cinnamon, anise, nutmeg, and vanilla sugar. On Advent Sundays she entertains around the lighted candles of their Advent wreath. Her home is always open to foreign guests.

It was on such a Sunday we sat together singing carols in English and German and talking of the delights of Swiss Christmas baking. Since then, *Mailänderli* have been a family favorite.

Mailänderli supposedly come from Milan, but people there are not familiar with the cookie. When you try them, you'll know what they miss!

Christmas Cookie Index

189

FESTIVE BREADS of CHRISTMAS

The fragrance of freshly baked coffee bread has ushered in the Christmas season for generations. In many countries, bread takes on a religious significance at Christmas and Easter. No holiday is complete without a festive bread—rich in eggs, sweet in butter, and laden with fruit and nuts.

This is a collection of Christmas bread recipes from many countries, lovingly shared by friends, gathered from aunts, mothers, and grandmothers. The foreign name of the recipe has been retained to provide a sense of the past.

*To my dear daughter, Susan, with the hope
that you may one day carry on this old
tradition of baking Christmas bread.*

Special thanks to Adaline Karber, who caters wedding receptions in San Jose, California, and to Samuel Kirk, career counselor and bread baking instructor, Denver, Colorado, for testing and evaluating Christmas bread recipes.

Thanks to Ellen Jane Price, teacher, and friend, for illustrating and decorating the pages in this series of holiday books, and to my husband, Alden, for encouragement, as well as eating and critiquing Christmas baking seven days a week.

Gratitude to Catherine Weidner (Moravians); Kaethe Warkentin, Bertha Harder (Russian Mennonites); Marthe Nussbaumer (Alsace); Margaret Kulish (Austria); Terttu Gilbert (Finland); Doris Walter, Elisabeth Mödlhammer (Germany); Kristina Scamagus (Greece); Iren Romoda (Hungary); Matilde Oliverio (Italy); Liesel Widmer, Erika Nussbaumer, Lilly Gyger, the baking staff of the Bienenberg Bible School (Switzerland); Liz Nelson (Norway); Margit Carlson (Sweden); Sonja Los Shore (Ukraine).

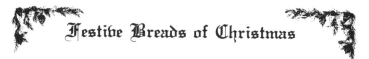

Festive Breads of Christmas

Our great-grandmothers, like generations of busy women before them, baked literally tons of dark, wholesome bread. Families were large. There were no corner bakeries. So bread was routinely baked at home—through good times and bad.

However, on holidays, especially Christmas and Easter, bread became more than nourishment—it became part of the family celebration.

From the pantry women brought their finest white flour (considered a luxury), gathered the freshest eggs from the barn, dipped generously into their butter churns, carried from the attic choicest dried fruits and nuts stored from harvest. They took saffron and spice from the cupboard.

Not enough, these extravagant ingredients. Women added yet another message: The shape of the bread must tell something of the religious meaning of the day. German mothers formed *Stollen* and *Fatschenkinder* to resemble a swaddling child. Ukrainians braided a royal three-tiered *Kolach*, ancient symbol of the Trinity and eternity. To the finished loaves they added a sprinkling of sugar or nuts, sculptured delicate flowers, birds, or a cross made from the dough.

Our great-grandmothers baked festive breads not as a chore, but with great joy. Sometimes they carried their bread to church to be blessed. To all they proclaimed: My gift of bread belongs to this holy season. It, too, is set apart from the simple, ordinary fare of every day.

On Christmas Eve the women proudly placed their loaves in the center of the table on the finest embroidered cloth, reserved for such days.

For centuries these beautiful breads have been a part of the Christmas season, adding dignity and meaning to the days of celebration. May they bring pleasure in your home as they do in ours.

Norma Jost Voth
San Jose, California

The Moravian Lovefeast

Moravian families look forward to a special children's lovefeast in their churches on Christmas Eve. In the tradition of the early church, they celebrate a "feast of love"—worship, music, and a simple meal together several times a year. Baskets of buns and mugs of coffee are served to everyone during the congregational singing.

Catherine Weidner recalls a time "when even the very young children were allowed to drink the mug of coffee at the lovefeast.... For as devoted Moravian parents said, 'Lovefeast coffee never hurt anyone!' It was quite a treat to be so 'grown up' several times a year. Now the children are served a cookie and mugs of chocolate milk.

"One of the three candle vigils on Christmas Eve is designated as the children's lovefeast. Lighted candles, symbols of Christian love and light, are passed to everyone in the congregation."

Catherine Weidner, Bethlehem, Pennsylvania, shares an old family recipe (p. 198) for these traditional Moravian Lovefeast Buns.

Moravian Lovefeast Buns

Candlelight lovefeasts, commemorating the birth of Christ, have been a tradition of the Moravian Church for more than 200 years. The first American lovefeast and candle service was held in Pennsylvania in 1756. Lovefeast buns and coffee are served to the congregation on Christmas Eve.

1 cup hot, dry mashed
  potatoes, unseasoned
2 pkg. active dry yeast
½ cup lukewarm water
1 tsp. sugar
½ cup butter
1 cup sugar

½ cup lukewarm milk
2 eggs, beaten
¼ tsp. nutmeg
½-1 tsp. mace
2 tbsp. grated orange
  peel
2 tbsp. orange juice
5-5½ cups flour

Pare, slice, and boil 2 or 3 potatoes. Mash and cool to luke-warm. (You may also use 1 cup prepared dry, quick, mashed potatoes.) Dissolve yeast in warm water and sugar. Cream butter and sugar together. Add mashed potatoes and mix well. Add lukewarm milk, eggs, yeast, seasonings, orange juice, and peel; mix well. Gradually add 2½ cups sifted flour and beat 5 minutes with electric mixer. Gradually add 2¼-2½ cups flour.

198

Turn out onto floured board and knead until smooth and elastic, about 8-10 minutes. Place in greased bowl, turning to grease top of dough. Cover with plastic wrap and let rise in warm place until doubled in bulk (about 1½ hours). Punch down and let rise a second time (40-45 minutes). Punch down.

Pinch off balls of dough (3 oz.) about the size of golf balls. Form into bun shape and place on greased baking sheet about 1½ inches apart. Flatten slightly. Cover with kitchen towel and let rise in warm place until doubled in size. Brush tops with melted butter or 1 egg beaten with 1 tsp. water. Bake at 350° about 15 minutes or until golden brown. Cover with towel to cool and soften. Makes 1½ dozen large buns.

COME LORD JESUS
OUR GUEST TO BE
AND BLESS THESE
GIFTS BESTOWED
by THEE. Amen

Russian Peppernuts

Grandmother called these coffee buns Russian Peppernuts. Russian—because it was one of the recipes her family brought from the Molotschna Colony (Ukraine) in Russia when the Mennonites settled on the plains of Kansas in 1874.

Traditionally the buns were sweetened with the much-loved watermelon syrup, plentiful because watermelons grew profusely in the rich Ukrainian soil. Hence they are also called Syrup Peppernuts, especially among the Mennonites in Canada. (Dark corn syrup and molasses have since replaced watermelon syrup.)

"My grandmother's peppernuts were raised with yeast, were high, light, and placed close together on the pan," says Miriam Penner Schmidt. From the yeast leavening they take another name—*Häv Päpanät*, Low German for Yeast Peppernuts.

200

The peppernut Christmas cookie tradition probably came with the Mennonites when they migrated from Holland to West Prussia to the Ukraine. Peppernut buns use some of the traditional cookie spices (often cinnamon and black pepper°) but are raised with yeast.

After the famine (1920s) in Russia, sugar, butter, cream—all the good baking ingredients—were scarce. Women baked their delicacies with whatever was available. "Mother flavored hers with fennel from the garden. If she was feeling particularly luxurious, she might brush the tops with a little egg," remembers Kaethe Kasdorf Warkentin.

These simple, tasty coffee buns, a unique ethnic product of Russian Mennonite kitchens, are baked not only at Christmas but year-round as well.

° Earlier pepper was the most expensive and highly prized of spices. The term pepper was used to mean not only black peppercorns but other spices as well.

Suse Toews' Russian Peppernuts

A Christmas specialty of Russian Mennonite kitchens, these high, light, spicy coffee buns bring back a host of nostalgic memories. The recipe comes from Suse Toews, Asuncion, Paraguay.

1 cup milk
½ cup margarine
½ cup brown sugar
½ tsp. salt
1½ pkg. active dry yeast
½ cup lukewarm water
2 tsp. sugar

½ cup dark Karo syrup
  or molasses
½ tsp. cinnamon
½ tsp. white pepper
¾ tsp. ground star anise°
4½-5 cups flour
Powdered Sugar Frosting

Over medium heat, blend milk, margarine, sugar, salt. Add syrup or molasses. Cool to lukewarm. Dissolve yeast in warm water and sugar. Combine milk and yeast mixtures. Add spices. Gradually add 2½ cups sifted flour and beat 5 minutes with electric mixer. Gradually add 2-2½ cups flour. Turn out onto floured board and knead until smooth and elastic, about 8-10

°You may substitute 1 tsp. crushed anise seed or 1 tsp. anise extract.

minutes. Place in greased bowl, turning to grease top of dough. Cover with plastic wrap and set in warm place to rise until doubled in bulk. Punch down. Pinch off balls of dough the size of large golf balls. Shape into buns and place close together on greased baking pans. Cover and let rise in warm place until doubled in size. Brush with melted margarine. Bake at 375° for 25-30 minutes or until golden brown. Cool on rack and cover with towel to soften. Makes 2½ dozen large buns.

Powdered Sugar Frosting: Combine 1 cup sifted confectioners' sugar, 1½ tbsp. milk, and ½-1 tsp. maple or vanilla flavoring.

o   o   o

Suse Toews is one of the many heroic women who suffered through World War II. After losing her father, husband, and brother in Russia, Mrs. Toews shepherded her aged mother, her brother's crippled wife, and five little children on foot from Russia to Germany, where she lived and cooked for refugees in a camp. Later in her new home in Paraguay, she continued cooking at the Mennonite Central Committee headquarters in Asuncion, all the while caring for her mother and raising her nieces and nephews. Now in her 70s, Mrs. Toews still cooks, bakes, and regularly sings in the church choir. A sample of her baking is the recipe above.

How Beautiful It Was!

"I remember one year we went to the church Christmas program by sleigh. Dad filled it with straw and we children crawled under buffalo robes and wool comforters," reflects (Aunt) Minnie Jost Krause, Hillsboro, Kansas. "Mother sat up front beside Dad, with the baby in her arms. I lay there, looking up at the stars, thinking about the program, and listening to the sleigh bells in the quiet night. How beautiful it was!

"At church each of us received gift sacks filled with candy, nuts, cookies, an orange, and apple. On the way home we were counting and smelling our treats when the horses hit a big drift, floundered, and the sleigh tipped over. All we children worried about was our candy. Nothing else mattered!... On New Year's Day they dismantled the big tree at church, and of course, we couldn't miss that, so we walked to town along the railroad tracks to be there. We usually came home with an orange, a cookie, or a string of popcorn from the tree."

Adaline Karber's Christmas Tree Bread

A spectacular centerpiece that's easy to make and serve. Mrs. Karber, who professionally caters receptions, frequently offers this festive tree for holiday breakfasts.

1 tbsp. instant potato
   flakes
⅓ cup boiling water
2 tsp. salt
1¼ cups milk
⅔ cup margarine
3 tbsp. sugar
1 tsp. nutmeg or 1 tsp.
   cardamom
2 tsp. grated orange peel
1 egg, beaten
4½ cups flour
1½ tbsp. yeast
Candied cherries
Glaze

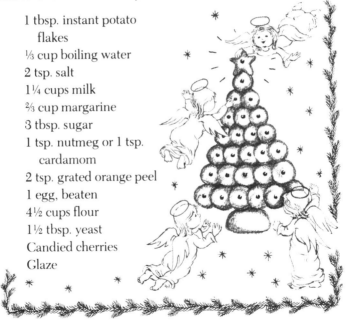

Combine potato, boiling water, and salt, and mix as for mashed potatoes. Scald milk; add margarine, sugar, spice. Cool to lukewarm and combine with potato. Add orange peel and egg and mix. Gradually add 2 cups sifted flour and yeast to milk mixture. Beat until smooth. Cover and set in warm place for 10 minutes. Gradually add remaining flour. Turn onto lightly floured board and knead until smooth and elastic, about 8-10 minutes. Place in greased bowl, turning to grease top of dough. Cover with plastic wrap and set in warm place until doubled in bulk. Punch down.

On lightly floured board, roll dough out to ½-inch thickness. Cut 26 circles with 2-inch cookie cutter and 1 star. Reserve small piece of dough to make a tree base. Line 12×15-inch baking sheet with parchment. To begin tree, place 6 circles in a row, *overlapping slightly*. Lay 5 circles twice to form rows above, then 4, then 3, 2, 1, always overlapping. Place star on top. Press out base for tree to 5×2½×3 inches and place under bottom row. Place ½ candied cherry in center of each circle. Cover and let rise in warm place 15-20 minutes. Do not let rise to double. Brush with 1 egg beaten with 1 tbsp. water. Bake at 350° for 25 minutes or until golden brown. Brush with egg wash once more. Brush with 1 cup white Karo syrup brought to boiling point. Cool on rack. (Use leftover dough to make a few dinner rolls.)

Festive Apricot Braid

A delicate coffee bread, braided over a colorful filling of apricots and maraschino cherries makes this a royal offering for holiday guests.

¾ cup milk
⅓ cup butter or
    margarine
½ cup sugar
1 tsp. salt
1 pkg. active dry yeast
¼ cup lukewarm water
1 tsp. sugar
3 eggs
1 tsp. grated lemon peel
4¼-4½ cups flour
Apricot/Cherry Filling

In a saucepan combine milk and butter over medium heat until very warm. Stir in sugar and salt. Cool to lukewarm. Sprinkle yeast over water and sugar. Beat eggs in mixer bowl. Add lukewarm milk/butter mixture, yeast, and lemon peel. Gradually add 2 cups sifted flour and beat 5 minutes with electric mixer.

Gradually add 2 cups flour. Turn out onto lightly floured board and knead until smooth and elastic, 8-10 minutes, using extra flour as necessary. Place in greased bowl, turning to grease top of dough. Cover with plastic wrap and let rise in warm place until doubled in bulk. Prepare Apricot/Cherry Filling.

Punch dough down. Turn out onto lightly floured board and knead lightly. Divide dough in half. Roll one piece into an 8×14-inch rectangle. Transfer to greased baking sheet. Spread ½ prepared filling down center third of rectangle. Cut 1-inch-wide strips along both sides of filling, cutting from filling to outer edges of dough. Fold strips at an angle, crisscross, over filling. Repeat with remaining dough. Cover with kitchen towel and let rise in warm place until doubled in size. Brush with 1 egg beaten with 1 tsp. water. Bake at 375° for 20-25 minutes or until golden brown. Cool. Drizzle with icing.

Apricot/Cherry Filling: Combine 2½ cups (11 oz. package) chopped, dried apricots and 1½ cups water in saucepan. Bring to a boil; cook until all liquid is absorbed. Stir in ¾ cup packed brown sugar. Cool. Add 1 cup finely chopped, well-drained maraschino cherries and ½ cup chopped blanched almonds or walnuts. (Variation: Add ½ cup well-drained crushed pineapple.)

Icing: 1 cup powdered sugar, 1½ tbsp. hot water, 2-3 drops almond extract.

Christmas Breakfast Wreath

Red and green cherries, raisins, and nuts lend a decorative look to this holiday wreath.

½ cup milk
¼ cup butter
¼ cup sugar
1 tsp. salt
1 pkg. active dry yeast

¼ cup lukewarm water
1 tsp. sugar
3 eggs
¼ tsp. cardamom
3½-4 cups flour

In a saucepan over medium heat combine milk, butter, sugar, and salt until very warm. Cool to lukewarm. Sprinkle yeast over lukewarm water and sugar. Beat eggs in mixer bowl. Add cardamom, yeast, and milk/butter mixture. Gradually add 2 cups sifted flour and beat 5 minutes with electric mixer. Gradually add 1½ cups flour and turn out onto lightly floured board and knead until smooth and elastic, about 8-10 minutes. Add flour as necessary to prevent sticking. Place in greased bowl, turning to grease top of dough. Cover with plastic wrap and set in warm place until doubled in bulk.

Punch dough down and turn onto lightly floured board. Roll dough into a 10×30-inch rectangle. Sprinkle filling over dough, leaving a 1-inch edge. Roll dough up tightly from long end.

Seal edges and ends. With a knife, cut roll in half lengthwise. Turn cut sides up. Loosely braid ropes, keeping cut sides up. Transfer to greased baking sheet. Shape into 12-inch circle. Pinch ends together securely. Let rise in warm place until doubled in size. Brush with butter. Bake at 375° about 20 minutes or until golden brown. Cool. Drizzle with glaze of 1 cup powdered sugar, 2 tsp. each lemon juice and milk.

Filling: Beat together ¼ cup *each* butter and flour, 2 tbsp. sugar, ¼ cup almond paste, 1 tsp. grated lemon peel, ½ tsp. almond extract. Stir in ⅔ cup finely chopped blanched almonds, ¼ cup *each* red and green chopped candied cherries, ⅓ cup golden raisins.

Abundantly Alsatian

A visit to Marthe Nussbaumer's Alsatian home, Schweighof, is certain to include a gastronomic feast. In her spacious, sunny farm kitchen she combines a blend of French and German cuisines in her own creative Alsatian-style cooking. Baking is routine there, but at Christmas she deftly adds twenty different varieties of tiny, delicate cookies, a half-dozen breakfast braids, rolls, and a parade of elegant tortes and desserts. Her Christmas menus (opposite) deserve their own three-star awards.

Traditionally, the Nussbaumers share Christmas Eve supper and then a quiet, intimate Holy Evening with their family. It is a time of gratitude and reflection on the year's blessings. Even now, as young adults, the children present a program of French carols—singing, flute, piano—for their parents.

Marthe and husband, Roland, live on a large model farm in the picturesque rolling countryside near Altkirch. Hers is a busy life of homemaking, church activity, managing the large, old eighteen-room Nussbaumer family home, and extra weekend cooking for children and friends returning to Schweighof from work and study in the city. In summer Marthe raises a profusion of flowers, tends a vegetable garden, and frequently entertains tour groups visiting their farm.

212

Christmas Eve Supper at Schweighof

Crudités

*Marinated Carrots, Beets,
Celery Root, French Green Beans,
Tomatoes & Onions*

*Winter Nüssli Salad
Vinaigrette Dressing*

Baked Ham in Pastry Casing

*Variety of French Provincial Cheeses
Crusty French Bread*

*Flaming "Norwegian Omlette"
(Baked Alaska Torte)
Christmas Cookies*

Coffee with Whipped Cream

Christmas Day Dinner at Schweighof

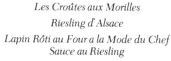

Les Croûtes aux Morilles

Riesling d'Alsace

*Lapin Rôti au Four a la Mode du Chef
Sauce au Riesling*

*Knöpfli
Salade Verte (Doucette) à la Vinaigrette*

*Glace à la Vanille Maison
Framboises Chaudes à la Liqueur*

Bûche de Noël

Rumtopf

*Petits Fours Maison
Café-Crème Chantilly*

Breakfast Braid (Zopf)

The perfect combination with butter and homemade jam, this high, golden braid is baked both in Alsace and Switzerland. Erika Nussbaumer, Basel, shares her recipe.

1 cup milk	¼ cup lukewarm water
5 tbsp. butter	1 tsp. sugar
1 tsp. salt	4 cups flour
1 pkg. active dry yeast	Egg Glaze

In a saucepan combine milk, butter, and salt over medium heat until very warm. Cool to lukewarm. Dissolve yeast in water and sugar. Combine yeast and milk/butter mixture in mixer bowl. Gradually add 2 cups sifted flour and beat 5 minutes with electric mixer. Gradually add remaining flour. Turn out onto floured board and knead until smooth and elastic, about 8-10 minutes. Place in greased bowl, turning to grease top of dough. Cover with plastic wrap and set in warm place until doubled in bulk. Punch down. Divide into 3 equal pieces. Roll each piece into a 20-inch rope and braid, pinching ends together. Place on greased baking sheet. Cover with kitchen towel and set in warm place until almost doubled in size. Brush with 1 egg beaten with 1 tsp. water. Bake at 400° for 15 minutes. Reduce

heat to 350° for another 15 minutes or until bread is hollow
sounding when tapped. Cool on rack and cover with towel to
soften. Makes 1 braid.

Austrians deck the halls—and all the other rooms—with
boughs of evergreen. Before Christmas, living-room doors
remain locked, sometimes for days. It is an old tradition that
angels work inside, preparing for the coming of the Holy Child
who brings the Christmas tree with all the candles and gifts
spread below its branches.

A TINY SILVER BELL tinkled outside the Trapp family's living room—the signal that the long-awaited moment, Christmas Eve, had arrived. Brimming with excitement, the children rushed down the long staircase of their Tyrolean home to the large festive parlor where, for the first time, they saw their Christmas tree, bright with more than a hundred lighted candles. It was the youngest of the children who came forward and recited, from memory, the Christmas story from the Bible. Then a hushed singing of "Stille Nacht" (Silent Night)," handshakes, hugs, kisses, and many a wish for "a blessed Christmas."

After supper and hasty naps, Baron Von Trapp, the first to awaken, stood with lantern in hand at the foot of the dark stairway, beckoning his children in song:

Shepherds quickly waken from your sleep,
The Good Shepherd is now awake.

From the top of the stairs they came in procession, each child carrying a flickering lantern and singing. Gathered below, they formed a choir:

Hurry, oh hurry and gifts you bring;
Come and adore Him, the Little King.

Then it was off to church with lanterns lighting the dark, snowy path as they joined their neighbors in a joyous midnight celebration.

216

CZECH FARMERS gladly share part of the Christmas Eve meal with their faithful animals. Even bees and fruit trees may be given special offerings of food and drink—in hope of a good harvest. All that lives and grows on the farm must share in this meal to ensure prosperity in the coming year.

Czechoslovakian Vánočka

A delectable breakfast or dessert bread for the Christmas holidays. The Czechs call it Van-*och*-ka.

¾ cup milk	3 egg yolks
½ cup sweet butter	Grated peel of ½ lemon
⅔ cup sugar	4-4½ cups flour
1 tsp. salt	¾ cup golden raisins
2 pkg. active dry yeast	½ cup chopped blanched
½ cup lukewarm water	almonds
2 tsp. sugar	Egg Glaze
	Sliced almonds

Combine milk and butter over medium heat until very warm. Stir in sugar and salt. Sprinkle yeast over water and sugar and dissolve. Beat egg yolks in mixer bowl; add lemon peel, yeast, and milk/butter mixtures. Gradually add 2 cups sifted flour and beat 5 minutes with electric mixer. Gradually add 2 cups flour and turn out onto lightly floured board. Use additional flour as necessary. Knead until smooth and elastic, about 8-10 minutes. Work in raisins and almonds evenly. Place in greased bowl, turning to grease top of dough. Cover with plastic wrap and set in warm place until doubled in bulk. Punch down.

Divide dough in half. Cut first half in 3 equal pieces. Cut remaining half in 4 equal pieces. Allow dough to rest 10 minutes. Roll 3 largest pieces into 18-inch rolls. Braid and pinch ends together. Place on greased baking sheet.

Roll 3 of the smaller pieces to 16-inch rolls and braid. Pinch ends together and place smaller braid on top of larger braid. Take remaining single portion of dough and divide in half. Roll into 2 18-inch strips. Twist strips together, rope-style. Place twist on top of smaller braid, tucking ends under larger braid. Cover and let rise in warm place until almost doubled in size. Brush with 1 egg slightly beaten with 1 tsp. water. Sprinkle with sliced almonds. Bake at 350° 35-40 minutes or until bread is hollow sounding on bottom when tapped. Cool.

Vánočka may also be iced with ¾ cup sifted powdered sugar, 2-3 tsp. milk, ⅛ tsp. almond extract. If icing, retain sliced almonds for sprinkling over frosting.

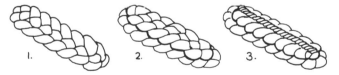

In Czechoslovakia, Christmas Eve is known as Štědrý Večer— the very rich night—because there are so many gifts and good things to eat.

TIP: "When stacking braided breads, do NOT put any butter or oil on the braids. Stand over the loaf(ves) when stacking, being sure to place each loaf directly on top each other. If not squarely centered, pick it up and move it until it is," says bread baking instructor, Sam Kirk. "If loaves slip during oven rise (watch carefully during the first five minutes of baking), then open the oven door, take out the baking sheet, and without hesitation, move the loaf(ves) around until it/they are centered again."

YOUR FUTURE IN A NUTSHELL. According to a quaint Czech tradition, young people play fortunetelling games on Christmas Eve. They simply float a nutshell with a lighted candle in a tub of water. If the shell moves toward the center of the tub, the owner goes on a trip. If the shell hovers near the rim, there's no journey in store. Should two shells float toward each other? A wedding's in the offing. Floating away—there's a year's delay.

"CRISPY APPLE STRUDEL, cookies, and a variety of Christmas rolls filled Mother's large cut-glass tray on Christmas Eve," remembers Lubuska Jerebek of her childhood in Prague. "The tray was left on the table for nibbling and quickly refilled when guests arrived."

For superstitious reasons, Mother never served "meat with feathers" for our Christmas meal. She maintained our good luck might fly away!

In our house there was a lot of singing. We children performed for our parents with guitar and piano. Most of the songs were spontaneous, with Mother starting a carol and everyone chiming in.

Dutch New Year's Olliebollen

This version of *Olliebollen* (sometimes called *Olykoeks*) allows you to serve fresh, warm fritters for a New Year's Day breakfast.

⅓ cup lukewarm milk	1 tsp. salt
1 pkg. active dry yeast	2¼ cups flour
¼ cup lukewarm water	1½ cups raisins and
1 tsp. sugar	currants
1 egg	1 tart apple, chopped

Heat milk to lukewarm. Dissolve yeast in water and sugar. Beat egg in mixer bowl. Add salt, yeast mixture, and milk. Gradually add sifted flour. Beat about 5 minutes with electric mixer. Add raisins and apple. Cover bowl with plastic wrap. Let stand overnight in refrigerator. (Or let rise until doubled and bake immediately.) Next morning, let stand in warm place to finish rising. In an electric skillet or deep fat fryer, heat cooking oil to 375°. With 2 iced teaspoons, shape small portions of batter into balls. Turn when golden brown. Drain on paper towels. Roll in sugar. Serve warm.

Tip: Chill spoons overnight in freezer.

222

When Johanna Hekkert, Sunnyvale, California, makes *Ollie-bollen* on New Year's Day, she makes *Appelflappen* at the same time. Apple slices, dipped in egg batter, are fried to golden perfection, sprinkled with sugar, and eaten as fast as she can fry them.

o   o   o

Among the early Dutch settlers in New York State's Hudson Valley it was customary to hold open house on New Year's Day. Good food (including *Olliebollen*) and good fellowship abounded.

Young men were known to rush from house to house, challenging each other to see who could make the most calls—especially where there were young ladies. A measure of a girl's popularity depended on the number of eligible young bachelors on the guest list. Eventually Dutch families took out newspaper ads announcing the hours during which they would receive callers on that day.

THE NÜRNBERG CHRISTKINDLESMARKT (Christ Child's Market) is thought to be the oldest Christmas fair in Germany. Its 400-year-old tradition, charming decorations, and myriads of lights in the old city all blend together in a captivating atmosphere for thousands of visitors. The market is really its own little town, spreading over the cobblestone square between the *Frauenkirche* (Church of Our Lady) and the beautiful old fountain, *Schöne Brunnen*.

More than 200 red-striped, canopied stalls offer a dazzling array of things to celebrate—the tiniest of handmade ornaments . . . wooden soldier nutcrackers . . . old-fashioned prune dolls. Vendors beckon you to sample their juicy *Bratwurst* and crunchy rolls. Burnt almonds . . . mountains of Fruit Bread . . . heaps of freshly baked *Lebkuchen* (honey cookies) . . . marzipan candies . . . all tempt you from stall to stall.

There a shepherds' choir plays from the steps of the *Frauenkirche*. . . . At the bakery corner an organ grinder in a red St. Nicholas suit cranks out "O Tannenbaum. . . ." For the children, there is a puppet theater . . . for adults, organ concerts and Christmas oratorios in the church.

The ancient crafts of skilled Nürnberg artists . . . the lovely Christmas music . . . the delicious—but crazy—mixture of foods . . . all make this market an exciting December adventure.

224

Traditional Früchtebrot/Kletzenbrot
(Fruit Bread)

Kletze (Klay-tze), a word used by farmers, means pear. Known also as *Hutzelbrot* and *Birnenbrot* (pear bread), this old German favorite is laden with moist dried fruits and nuts. Hundreds of loaves of Fruit Bread are sold daily at the Nürnberg Christ Child's Market during the Advent season. Lilly Gyger, Füllinsdorf, Switzerland, shares a very old family recipe.

1 cup (6 oz.) dried
    pears, halved
¾ cup pitted prunes,
    coarsely chopped
1 cup golden raisins
1 cup dark raisins
¾ cup figs, halved
½ cup whole almonds
1¼ cups walnut halves
¾ cup whole filberts
¾ cup candied orange
    peel
2 tbsp. vanilla°

2 tbsp. lemon juice
2 tbsp. grated lemon peel

Bread Dough
¾ cup milk
½ cup sweet butter
2 tbsp. active dry yeast
¼ cup lukewarm water
1 tbsp. sugar
1 tsp. salt
1 tsp. *each* coriander,
    mace, ground anise seed
2 cups flour

Cover pears with water and cook slightly. (Do not overcook or pears become mushy.) Drain. Cool. Pat dry. Cover prunes with hot water and allow to stand briefly. Cool. Drain and pat dry. Wash and dry raisins. Combine all remaining fruits and nuts in large bowl. Sprinkle with vanilla, lemon juice, and peel. °(European bakers sprinkle fruit with 2 tbsp. *Kirschwasser*.) Let fruit stand while preparing bread dough, or for several hours. Stir fruit occasionally.

In a saucepan combine milk and butter over medium heat until very hot. Cool to lukewarm. Sprinkle yeast over water and sugar to dissolve. Combine milk/butter and yeast mixtures; add salt and spices. Gradually work in sifted flour and beat 5 minutes with electric mixer. Cover with plastic wrap and set in warm place until doubled in bulk. Punch dough down.

Knead dough into bowl of fruit, distributing evenly. Spoon into 2 well-greased 4½×7½-inch loaf pans. Cover and let rise in warm place until doubled in size, about 2-3 hours. Brush with water. Garnish with blanched almond halves and candied cherries. Bake at 325° 1 hour or until done. Brush with water several times while baking. Remove from pans and cool. Wrap in aluminum foil. Age at least 1 week before slicing. Fruit Bread improves greatly with age. Serve with butter.

This bread looks rather "rough" and plain. It may be glazed or brushed with white Karo syrup while still warm.

Mother used to dry fruits from the garden down in the lower basement, remembers Margaret Kulish of her childhood home in Austria. Bunches of grapes were cut fresh from the vine in the late summer afternoon when they had cooled from the heat of the sun. Dried on the stem, they were sweet as plums. Apple slices, succulent with sugar, were strung like beads on white thread to dry for winter baking. We also had pears. Mother's fruit had a lovely aroma and a very distinct flavor I don't find in commercially dried fruits.

o   o   o

German farm women dried their orchard fruit in big outdoor ovens after bread baking. Later it was stored in baskets in the attic. Choicest dried pears, grapes, and plums they saved for the Christmas Fruit Bread/*Kletzenbrot*.

o   o   o

Austrian women used knitting needles to poke holes in the *Kletzenbrot* (pear bread)—then poured in *Mirabella Schnaps* (yellow plum liqueur) for extra flavor and good keeping.

Bunte Teller

The custom of Bunte Teller, a brightly colored dish laden with fruit, nuts, and homebaked cookies, originated in Germany.

Early on Christmas Eve, Mother covered the table with her best cloth and we children set out special deep plates to be filled with nuts and candies. My plate, white with a deep pink fluted edge, came from Russia.... Later we went to bed and tried hard to sleep, but couldn't. In the stillness we'd hear a clink, clink, clink from the dining room. This was Dad, putting the peanuts, nuts, and candies on our plates. Beside the plate they put a little gift. One in particular I remember—a little purse with a tiny mirror in the lid. All my friends at church envied me on Christmas morning. (Bertha Fast Harder is a Christian education instructor in Elkhart, Indiana.)

German Christstollen

The baking of Christmas *Stollen* is another ancient German custom, originating in Dresden about 1400. In those days people tried to represent biblical ideas in baking. Many old cookie forms and molds depict familiar Bible stories. The *Stollen* form represents the Christ Child in swaddling clothes.

Stollen is traditionally rich in butter, raisins, almonds, and citron; the top is generously dusted with confectioners' sugar. This bread is served in every German home at Christmas.

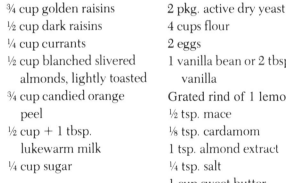

¾ cup golden raisins
½ cup dark raisins
¼ cup currants
½ cup blanched slivered almonds, lightly toasted
¾ cup candied orange peel
½ cup + 1 tbsp. lukewarm milk
¼ cup sugar

2 pkg. active dry yeast
4 cups flour
2 eggs
1 vanilla bean or 2 tbsp. vanilla
Grated rind of 1 lemon
½ tsp. mace
⅛ tsp. cardamom
1 tsp. almond extract
¼ tsp. salt
1 cup sweet butter

Prepare fruit and nuts in a bowl. (Optional: Sprinkle with ¼ cup rum or brandy and mix well. Let stand 1 hour. Drain fruit on paper towel and press dry.) Sprinkle with ¼ cup of the flour and toss.

Place warm milk, 2 tbsp. sugar, and yeast in a bowl. Beat in 1 cup sifted flour. Cover and let rise in warm place 20 minutes. Beat eggs and remaining sugar. Add vanilla bean seeds or vanilla extract, lemon peel, salt, cardamom, mace, and almond extract and mix well. Add sponge and mix. Gradually add 1 cup flour and beat 5 minutes with electric mixer or knead by hand until smooth and elastic. Cover with plastic wrap and set in warm place 15 minutes. *(Please turn page.)*

Margaret Kulish says it was traditional in Austria to make the motion of the cross three times with the knife before cutting the Stollen.

Combine remaining flour and butter as for pie crust. Knead into firm ball. Combine yeast dough and flour/butter dough. On lightly floured board knead the combined doughs until smooth and elastic. Cover with plastic wrap and let stand in warm place until doubled in bulk. Punch dough down. Gently knead in fruit and nuts, a small amount at a time, working carefully so as not to discolor dough; distribute fruit evenly. Divide dough in half. Lightly roll and pat dough to 8×12-inch oval. Brush with melted butter. Turn dough over lengthwise and seal in typical *Stollen* form (see picture). Repeat with remaining dough. Place *Stollen* on parchment-lined baking tins. Cover and let rise until doubled in size. (This is slow; allow enough time.) Brush each *Stollen* well with melted butter. Bake at 350° about 45 minutes or until hollow sounding when tapped with your knuckles. While warm, brush again with melted butter. Dust generously with sifted powdered sugar. Cool. Wrap in aluminum foil and store in a cool place to mellow for a week. Cut in thin slices and serve with sweet butter. *Stollen* lasts a long time if securely wrapped in foil in the refrigerator. (If making 1 large *Stollen*, bake for 60 minutes.)

"*Christstollen* is lighter than *Dresdenerstollen*," explains Masterbaker, Karl Kaestel, Nürnberg. "Both are rich in almonds, fruit, and spices," he says, "but it is the *zitronat* (citron) that gives the *Stollen* its 'certain joy.' "

Fatschen, the old German word meaning to wrap or bind, is still used in some parts of South Germany and Austria, says Elisabeth Mödlhammer. Earlier *Fatschenkinder*, made of wax or silver, were used as votive offerings. Baked as molded cookies or cakes, they were given as gifts to new mothers (a kind of "good health" greeting) and as wedding gifts, wishing the bride and groom to be richly blessed with children.

In the last bread baking before Christmas, Bavarian farm women used their better flour to make a *Christkindl* or *Fatschenkindl* to serve for a pre-Christmas meal. *Fatschenkinder*, baked in this ancient, simple form, still remind us of the infant Jesus, "wrapped in swaddling clothes and laid in a manger."

South German Fatschenkind

The world-famous Dallmeyer Delicatessen, Munich, Germany, has served kings and princes with a wide array of house specialties, exotic fruits from distant lands, and baking delights. One of their Christmas bakery offerings is the *Fatschenkind* (or *Wickelkind*), a breakfast bread shaped like a babe in swaddling clothes. Germans have baked cookies, cakes, or bread in this form since the 1600s.

¾ cup milk
⅓ cup butter
⅓ cup sugar
1 tsp. salt
1 pkg. active dry yeast

¼ cup lukewarm water
1 tsp. sugar
1 egg
4-4½ cups flour
Egg Glaze
Currants or raisins

Heat milk and butter until very warm. Add sugar and salt and mix. Cool to lukewarm. Dissolve yeast in water with sugar. Beat egg in mixer bowl. Add yeast and milk/butter mixtures. Gradually add 2 cups sifted flour and beat 5 minutes with electric mixer. Gradually add remaining 2 cups sifted flour.

Turn out onto lightly floured board and knead until smooth and elastic, about 8-10 minutes. Dough should not stick to the board. Place in greased bowl, turning to grease top of dough. Cover with plastic wrap and set in warm place until doubled in bulk. Punch dough down.

Small Fatschenkinder: Divide dough into 6 equal parts. (Cut a tiny piece of dough from each for decoration.) Roll each piece into a smooth 8-inch oblong. With the side of your hand, "cut" a head for each body, leaving it slightly attached to body (see p. 279, 1 and 2). Place *Fatschenkinder* on greased baking sheets. Flatten bodies and shape (see picture, p. 233). Cover with kitchen towel and let rise in warm place for 15 minutes. Meanwhile, add a little extra flour to each remaining piece of dough. Roll out into very long, thin strips for decoration. Brush each "child" with 1 egg beaten with 1 tsp. water. Lay decorative strip on "child" as illustrated on page 233. Brush strip with egg. Punch currants or raisins into each body for eyes, nose, and button decor. Let rise until doubled in bulk. Bake at 350° for 15-17 minutes or until hollow-sounding when tapped. Cool on rack and cover with towel to soften. Makes 6 *Fatschenkinder.*

Large Fatschenkind: Use entire piece of dough to make 1 large "child." Follow directions as above. Use whole blanched almonds for decoration.

Greek Advent Eftazymo

Efta in Greek means "seven." *Zymo*—knead. Bread kneaded seven times—that's *Eftazymo!*

Made during the Advent season, this pre-Christmas bread depends on an interesting combination of chick peas and wood ashes for leavening. The night before baking, Greek women grind chick peas, add salt, a sprinkling of wood ash, and hot water to a large pot. This is covered and set in a warm place to ferment overnight.

In the morning, foam from the peas is skimmed off and mixed with a half cup of flour and placed in a warm, sunny spot to rise. (If there is no foam, start the whole process again!) Foam and flour are added to the starter two more times; finally sugar, egg, anise, and remaining flour are added to make a dough.

Baked to a crusty golden brown, this bread of "seven kneadings" is a lot of work. But Greeks insist the flavor and aroma of *Eftazymo* are worth all the effort. For curious readers, here are the (untested) ingredients: 8 oz. chick peas, ½ tsp. salt, ½ tsp. wood ashes, 1¼ cups hot water, 9½ cups flour, 1 tsp. ground anise seed, ½ cup sugar, 1 egg, water to make soft dough. Yield: 2 large loaves.

"*CHRISTMAS IN OUR GREEK VILLAGE* had a special 'flavor,'" recalls Kristina Scamagus of San Jose, California. "There was heart and spirit in the celebration. Even though times were difficult and people worked very hard, I remember their smiling faces had real peace and joy."

Kristina's mother still bakes their traditional Christmas bread, *Christopsomo*. In her village families were large and on farms there were extra workers to cook for, so women baked from ten to twelve big loaves of *Christopsomo* at one time. "It was a lot of work, making the fire and heating up the big outdoor oven. You had to wait a long time for the temperature to be just right."

Greeks traditionally top *Christopsomo* with a cross. To this Kristina's mother adds birds, daisies, and flowers, all sculptured out of bread dough. "The bread was placed in the center of the table because the ladies were proud of their cheerful decorations."

Greek Christopsomo

(Christmas Bread)

Walnut halves and a cross decorate this ancient Christmas bread from Greece. The special flavoring is *masticha*.

½ cup milk
1 cup butter
⅔ cup sugar
1 tsp. salt
1-1½ tbsp. *masticha*°
   or 2 tsp. crushed
   anise seed
2 pkg. active dry yeast
½ cup lukewarm water
1 tsp. sugar
4 eggs
5½-6 cups flour

Pulverize masticha in blender or crush anise seeds with mortar and pestle. Combine milk, sugar, salt, butter, and *masticha* (or anise) and bring to a boil. Cool to lukewarm. Sprinkle yeast

---

°*Masticha* or gum mastic is a resin from the Mediterranean mastic tree, available in Middle Eastern delis and markets.

238

over water and 1 tsp. sugar and dissolve. Combine with luke-warm milk/butter mixture. Beat eggs in mixer bowl and add the milk/yeast mixture. Gradually add 1½ cups sifted flour to liquid. Beat 2 minutes with electric mixer. Gradually add 4 cups flour. Turn out onto lightly floured board and knead until smooth and elastic, about 8-10 minutes, adding last ½ cup flour as necessary. Place in greased bowl, turning to grease top of dough. Cover with plastic wrap and set in warm place until doubled in bulk. Punch down.

Turn dough onto floured board and knead lightly. Pinch off 2 pieces of dough, each about 3 inches in diameter. Set aside. Shape remaining dough into a round loaf, and place pucker side down on greased baking sheet. Flatten with palm of hand. Roll each of the small balls into 14-inch ropes. Cut a 5-inch slash at the end of each. Lay ropes on loaf, crossing ropes at center of loaf. Curl slashed ends away from the center, forming a small circle. Place walnut half in each circle and one in center of cross. Cover and let rise until doubled in size. Brush with slightly beaten egg white. (Optional: sprinkle with sesame seeds.) Bake at 350° for 45 minutes or until hollow sounding when tapped. Cool. Makes 1 large loaf.

Before cutting this loaf, the Greek father makes the sign of the cross with a knife and wishes everyone joy and health.

"*DECEMBER 6* is the beginning of our Christmas season in Hungary," says Iren Romoda. "On that day Mother often planted little plates of wheat seed which grew to about an inch and a half. The bright green was very nice when everything was gray and dreary outdoors. Sometimes she used it as the centerpiece for our Christmas dinner." (The memory of the wheat prompted Mrs. Romoda to revive this old tradition with her own family.)

"In South Hungary it was traditional to bring wheat straw into the house, spreading it around the room. Our mother never allowed us to do that; she thought it much too messy. But we children loved to play in it at the neighbors. Sometimes their presents got lost in the straw.

"Our big pastry in Hungary—and all the Slavic countries—is poppy seed roll. You're offered this treat wherever you go. We Hungarians joke about 'getting roll poisoning.' We also ate a lot of dried fruits during the holidays. Hard candies were made at home and wrapped in colored foil to hang on the tree. There was a lot of scrambling for those candies when the tree came down on January 6.

"Christmas Eve celebrations are very private. There are no presents—just a tree, candle, and much singing." (Mrs. Romoda teaches Slavic languages in Berkeley, California.)

MERRY CHRISTMAS! Say it with food. A loaf of sweet bread to a new neighbor. A plate of cookies for a lonely child. A cake says more than a handclasp. A recipe shared with a new friend is a link forever. These warm, human, get-to-know-you better gifts of love show that you care. Know someone who needs a lift? Say Merry Christmas—with a gift from your kitchen.

Hungarian Diós Kalács
(Walnut Roll)

Typical of Old World recipes is this walnut roll (*dee*-ohsh *kah-lahch*) brought to this country by grandmothers of Hungarian, Yugoslav, Croatian, and Russian backgrounds. A Slavic holiday favorite, the rich coffee bread is enhanced by a filling of ground nuts, honey, and raisins.

Dough
2 pkg. active dry yeast
½ cup lukewarm milk
2 tsp. sugar
¼ cup butter
½ cup sugar
½ tsp. salt
2 egg yolks
1 whole egg
½ cup sour cream
3½-4 cups flour

Walnut Filling
¼ cup butter
1 cup sugar
½ cup heavy cream
¼ cup honey
1 tsp. vanilla
3½ cups ground walnuts
1 tsp. cinnamon
1 cup golden raisins
Melted butter

Sprinkle yeast over warm milk and 2 tsp. sugar. Heat sour cream over low heat just to lukewarm. Cream butter and sugar; add eggs and beat well. Add warm sour cream, yeast, salt, and mix. Gradually add 1½ cups sifted flour. Beat 5 minutes with electric mixer. Gradually add 2 cups sifted flour. Turn out onto lightly floured board and knead until smooth and elastic, about 8-10 minutes. Use additional flour to keep dough from sticking. Place in greased bowl, turning to grease top of dough. Cover with plastic wrap and set in warm place until doubled in bulk.

Punch dough down, working out air bubbles. Divide dough in half. On lightly floured board, roll half of dough into a 12×12-inch square. Spread half of filling over dough to within 1 inch of edge. Sprinkle with half the cinnamon and raisins. Roll as for jelly roll. Pinch ends and seam together and turn under. Place seam side down on greased baking sheet. Repeat with remaining dough. Prick top of roll every 3 inches with fork to eliminate air bubbles. Brush with melted butter. Cover with kitchen towel and set in warm place to rise until doubled in size. Bake at 350° for 35-40 minutes or until done. If necessary, cover lightly with foil to prevent burning. Brush again with melted butter. Cool on wire rack. Wrap in foil. Freezes well. Makes 2 loaves. *(Please turn page.)*

Walnut Roll Filling: Plump raisins in hot water. Drain and pat dry. In a saucepan on low burner, melt butter. Stir in sugar, cream, honey, and bring to a boil. Add vanilla and walnuts. Cool. If filling is too thick to spread, add a little extra cream or milk.

Eithne Cuckel's father, Mayo County, Ireland, called Christmas Eve the night of the "Big Nuff"—the one night everyone had enough to eat.

Mary Sheridan's Irish Soda Bread

Mary's mother, Bridget Kelly, brought this recipe from Ireland where they baked soda bread in iron skillets on the open hearth. Mary still skillet-bakes the bread as regular fare for her family and presents it as gifts on holidays to friends in Santa Clara, California.

5 cups flour
1 tsp. soda
1½ tsp. baking powder
1 cup sugar
1 cup butter

1-¾ cups raisins
1½ tsp. caraway
2 tsp. grated orange
    peel (optional)
1 egg, slightly beaten
2½ cups buttermilk

Sift dry ingredients together. (You may use ½ whole wheat flour if desired.) Cut butter in small pieces and work into flour with your hands. Add raisins, caraway seed, and orange rind. Beat egg lightly; add buttermilk and pour into dry mixture. Mix well. Pour batter into large greased cast iron skillet or dutch oven; form into round ball. With a sharp knife, cut a cross in the center top. Bake at 350° for 60-75 minutes or until knife inserted in center comes out clean. Cool. Allow to stand 1 day before cutting.

Poems, Promises, & Presepe

When I was a schoolgirl in Naples, Italy, we wrote Christmas letters full of promises to our parents, relates Matilde Oliverio. Though this happened yearly, Father still expressed great surprise each time he "discovered" our epistles hidden under his napkin or plate at the dinner table. It was also customary for us to recite long, beautiful poems to our parents before dessert (*panettone, torrone, struffoli* ...) was served. Eel is the traditional meal for an Italian Christmas Eve. Chestnuts, too, are part of the meal—and many sweets.

In Italy the Christmas celebration centers around the *presepe* (crèche) with all its figures—often family heirlooms. We had family prayers around our *presepe* each morning.

There is a lovely candle ceremony practiced in some of our Italian villages: At the Christmas dinner the father lights a candle and passes it down through the family members until it reaches the youngest. If there is a baby, the mother holds the candle in the baby's hand and together they put it in the center of the table. If there is no baby, they blow it out and save it for next year's Christmas, hoping by then there will be a new baby! (Mrs. Oliverio shares holiday traditions in her Italian language classes in San Jose, California.)

247

Panettone

A light cake-bread eaten throughout Italy, especially at Christmas, with breakfast coffee. Legend tells that this fruity bread was created in Milan. In order to win the hand of the girl he loved, a young nobleman named Antonio hired himself to the girl's father, a baker. To make an impression and improve a waning business, Toni added butter and sugar to the bread dough, tossed in candied fruits and several dozen eggs. People liked his bread which became known as "Pane di Toni," or Toni's bread.

½ cup lukewarm milk
1 pkg. active dry yeast
¼ cup lukewarm water
1 tsp. sugar
¾ cup sweet butter
½ cup sugar
½ tsp. salt
5 egg yolks
1 whole egg

½ tsp. grated lemon peel
3½-4 cups flour
½ cup golden and dark
  raisins combined
½ cup blanched slivered
  almonds
¼ cup diced candied
  orange and lemon
  peel combined

(Optional: Plump raisins in a little brandy.) Heat milk to luke-warm. Dissolve yeast in warm water with sugar. Cream butter. Beat in sugar; add salt. Add egg yolks and whole egg, 1 at a time. Beat until smooth. Add 2 cups sifted flour. Beat 5 minutes with electric mixer. Stir in yeast, milk, and lemon peel. Gradually add remaining flour and turn out onto lightly floured board and knead until smooth, elastic, and no longer sticky, about 8-10 minutes. Gently work in raisins, almonds, and candied peel. Place in greased bowl, turning to grease top of dough. Cover with plastic wrap and let rise in warm place until doubled in bulk (about 3 hours).

Punch dough down. Turn onto lightly floured board and knead lightly. Divide in half. Shape into 2 round loaves about 6 inches in diameter. Place on greased baking sheet or in greased cake pans. Cover and let rise in warm place until doubled in size. Brush with melted butter or 1 egg beaten with 1 tsp. water. Cut cross in tops with sharp knife. Bake at 350° for 30 minutes or until golden brown. Cover with foil if necessary to prevent burning. Cool on wire rack. Slice and serve warm with butter.

LA BEFANA, a good little witch, was sweeping her house the night the wise men came by with presents for the Baby Jesus—so the legend goes. The kings invited the old woman to come with them to Bethlehem, but La Befana foolishly refused, saying she had work to do.

Later, broom still in hand, La Befana set out to catch up with them, but lost her way. She has never found the wise men, Bethlehem, or the *Bambino*. Every year she goes through Italy, searching, leaving presents for the good children on her way. Italian boys and girls eagerly await La Befana, writing letters and lists for their presents. On January 6 their stockings are filled—by La Befana.

251

Christmas Sleigh Rides

In Poland the days between Christmas and New Year were such merry, festive times. When I was a young girl there were moonlight sleigh rides with prancing horses and jingling bells.

Buried under lap robes and bundled in caps and mufflers, we sang and laughed our way from village to village. At least once during the evening, the driver made a sudden, sharp turn, dumping everyone into the cold, wet snow. A warm welcome—glowing hearth, honey cakes, and poppy seed rolls—awaited us at a friend's home where we sang and laughed some more.

During Christmas week people did as little work as possible, leaving plenty of time to celebrate, to enjoy their Christmas trees decked with apples, nuts, candies, hand-blown decorated eggs. There was a lot of visiting, eating, and singing. "Those times are among my fondest memories."—Shared by Wera Kawulka, who helps keep traditions alive in a South Bay (California) Polish Women's Organization.

A Polish Christmas Eve Supper

(Wigilia)

Pickled Herring in Sour Cream

Borscht without Meat

Pierogi—Cheese and Sauerkraut

Northern Pike

Fish and Horseradish Sauce

Pickled Beets

Noodles with Poppy Seed and Raisins

Poppy Seed Rolls

Christmas Bread

Light Fruitcake

Twelve Fruit Compote

*Christmas Eve supper begins when the first star appears
in the evening sky.*

Polish Poppy Seed Roll

Before the Christmas Eve meal, Polish families share a communion wafer, *oplatek*, a symbol of love, friendship, and forgiveness. One does not come to Christmas without forgetting and forgiving. Our supper is not lavish, but includes traditional dishes, among which is poppy seed roll, says Wera Kawulka. An extra plate is set for a stranger—who might be Christ.

Dough	*Poppy Seed Filling*
2 pkg. active dry yeast	2 cups poppy seeds
¼ cup lukewarm water	½ cup boiling milk
2 tsp. sugar	¾ cup sugar
¼ cup butter	2 tbsp. butter
½ cup sugar	2 tbsp. heavy cream
2 egg yolks	3 tbsp. honey
1 whole egg	2 tsp. grated orange peel
1 cup lukewarm sour cream	2 egg whites
½ tsp. salt	1 tart apple, grated, or
4-4½ cups flour	¼-½ cup golden raisins
Egg Glaze	(optional)

Sprinkle yeast over warm water and sugar. Heat sour cream over low heat just until lukewarm. Cream butter and sugar; add eggs and beat well. Add warm sour cream, yeast, salt, and mix. Gradually add 1½ cups sifted flour. Beat 5 minutes with electric mixer. Gradually add 2½ cups sifted flour. Turn out onto lightly floured board and knead until smooth and elastic, about 8-10 minutes. Use additional flour to keep dough from sticking. Place in greased bowl, turning to grease top of dough. Cover with plastic wrap and set in warm place until double in bulk. Punch dough down. Cover and let rise in warm place again until double in bulk.

Punch dough down. Divide in half. On lightly floured board, roll half of dough to 14×14 inch square. Spread half of filling over dough to within 1 inch of edge. Sprinkle with grated apple or raisins (optional). Carefully roll as for jelly roll. Pinch ends and seam together and turn under. Place seam side down on greased baking sheet. Repeat with remaining dough. Cover with kitchen towel and set in warm place until doubled in size. Brush with 1 egg beaten with 1 tsp. water. Bake at 350° for 40 minutes or until done. If necessary, cover lightly with foil to prevent burning. Cool. Wrap in foil. Freezes well. Makes 2 loaves.

Filling: (Optional: Plump raisins or grated apple.) Cover poppy seeds with boiling milk; cover and let steam 30 minutes. Grind. Combine sugar, cream, honey, butter, peel, and poppy seeds. Bring to a boil and cook 5 minutes over low heat. Cool. Beat egg whites until stiff. Gently fold in poppy seeds.

A Finnish Country Christmas

We choose our Christmas tree in summer while gathering wild blueberries in the woods near our home. When someone spots a tree that is round, full, and just the right height he shouts, "There's our Christmas tree!" (In winter when the trees are laden with snow, it is difficult to see their shape.) The tree is carefully marked and then early on the morning of December 24, Father and the boys go out and cut it. When it's dry, we bring the tree indoors to decorate.

On Christmas Eve everyone eagerly waits for the visit from *Joulupukki* (you-lo-poh-kay), our Finnish Santa Claus. He's a jolly fellow in red fur-trimmed suit and shiny black boots. Making a big noise with his stick he calls, "Where are all the good and obedient children in this house?" Father invites him in, offering a chair. *Joulupukki* tells of his sleigh ride from Lapland, about his workshop and calls us to sit on his knee, inquiring if we've been good. We are a little scared, yet curious. He asks if we've helped Mother. Do we tease each other or the cat? Actually, he already knows all about us from his little helpers, the *Joulutontut*, who peek in windows before Christmas. For those who've been obedient and good, there are gifts in his bag. Sometimes we sing and dance with him around the tree.

256

Now it's time for some of us to clean up the paper and ribbons from his presents while the others go for a Christmas *sauna* (sow-na, as the Finns say). Then there's dinner and finally it's time to light candles on the tree. In Finland we add Christmas sparklers—like Americans use on the Fourth of July. Because the tree is so fresh, we can hang them right on the branches. What a lovely sight to see, candles and sparklers lighting the dark room.

On Christmas Eve Father gives the animals extra straw and lots of hay to munch all night. Before going to bed, my parents go to the barn to feed them once more and wish these, our animal friends, a Merry Christmas.

Church is at 7:00 the next morning, but we must be up at least by 4:30 since we have two hours to go by sleigh. The night is dark and cold; stars are still out. Gladly we snuggle under Mother's warm woolen comforter, embroidered and decorated with bright pom-poms.

Our parish is large, the church building very old (300 years) and there is no heat. Often we must stand, for the sanctuary is packed. Our usually conservative pastor celebrates this special day in a white robe with festive colors. Daylight is just breaking when the service is over. Another two hours by sleigh and we return to a breakfast of ham, fruit soup with dried plums and raisins, and Mother's Christmas *pulla* (p. 260).

For us Finns, Christmas is a very quiet day. Children play with new toys, parents read new books, or even take a nap, since we were up very early. Dinner is served in the afternoon.

On St. Stephens' Day (December 26) there is a special childrens' church service. It is a cheerful, lively day—a day for play.

(Memories shared by Terttu Pujanen Gilbert of her childhood in Finland. She now lives in California.)

FINNISH FARM WIVES traditionally are great bakers. Their old-time ovens were built into a wall behind the stove, like a tunnel, about three feet wide and sometimes six feet deep.

At baking time, a wood fire was lit in the oven. When it had burned down, the red, glowing embers were raked to the front of the stove with a kind of shovel on a long pole. The women then brushed out the oven with a wet broom. A ventilator at the back of the stove drew off the smoke while a damper regulated the heat.

Heating the oven was a lot of work, as was mixing and kneading large batches of dough by hand. Usually they baked for the entire week. Terttu Gilbert says their big wood-burning stove had to be heated for two hours before baking. "When the heat was just right we first baked the bread, then cakes, and last the casseroles in the waning heat."

Finnish farm women still bake in large quantities, especially before Christmas, since no work is to be done during the Christmas week.

Finnish Christmas Pulla

"At Christmas Mother made *pulla* with cardamom and raisins. Sometimes she braided it into a wreath filled with jam and topped with almonds," recalls Terttu Gilbert. "Cardamom is our Christmas spice—saffron is for Easter. Mother always added extra cardamom to the *pulla* for Christmas. We children loved it with hot berry juice made from black currants and spices for afternoon tea."

1 cup milk
½ cup sweet butter
⅔ cup sugar
½ tsp. salt
1 pkg. active dry yeast
¼ cup lukewarm water

1 tsp. sugar
2 eggs
1 tsp. freshly ground
   cardamom
4½-5 cups flour
⅔ cup raisins (optional)
Sliced almonds (optional)

Combine milk and butter over medium heat until very warm. Stir in sugar and salt. Cool to lukewarm. Sprinkle yeast over water and sugar. Beat eggs. Add milk/butter and yeast mixtures and cardamom. Gradually add 2 cups sifted flour and beat 5 minutes with electric mixer. Gradually add 2½ cups additional flour. Turn out onto lightly floured board and knead until smooth and elastic, about 8-10 minutes. Dough should not stick to the board. Work in raisins if desired. Place in greased bowl, turning to grease top of dough. Cover with plastic wrap and set in warm place until doubled in bulk. Punch down.

Pulla Braid: To make 1 large braid, divide dough into 3 equal pieces. Roll each piece into an 18-inch-long rope. Braid. Seal ends. Place on greased baking sheet. Cover and let rise until doubled in size. Brush with slightly beaten egg white. Sprinkle with almonds if desired. Bake at 350° for 35-40 minutes or until done. Cool on rack and cover with terry cloth towel to soften.

Pulla Wreath: Divide dough in half. Roll out into 8×16-inch rectangle. Brush with melted butter. Spread with choice of fillings (p. 262). Roll as for jelly roll. Pinch ends. Place seam side down on greased baking sheet. Form into a wreath. Cut through roll at ¾-inch intervals. Pull and twist each slice to lay flat. Repeat with remaining dough or turn 2nd piece into *pulla* braid. Cover with kitchen towel and let rise in warm place until doubled in size. Brush wreaths with slightly beaten egg white. Sprinkle with sugar. Bake at 350° for 25-30 minutes or until done. Cool. Serve warm with butter. *(Please turn page.)*

Raspberry Filling for Pulla: ⅓ cup raspberry jam, ¼ cup finely chopped blanched almonds.

Raisin-Jam Filling for Pulla: ⅓ apricot jam or orange marmalade, ⅓ cup golden raisins, ¼ cup finely chopped blanched almonds.

"*MY FINNISH GRANDMOTHER* said they used to race to church in their sleighs on Christmas morning. The first family to arrive would be assured of a good harvest," says Martha Sonnenblick of Los Gatos, California.... Grandmother had another supersitition about the weather. If it was nice on Christmas Day, it would be nice all of January. The weather on the day after Christmas forecast the kind of weather we'd have in February.

"In Finland we often make baskets of spring flowers to give as Christmas gifts," adds Martha, "bright tulips, purple hyacinth, lily of the valley, and narcissus are some of the favorites."

SHOOTING IN CHRISTMAS had its origin back when Norwegian men used to fire shots out in the yard on Christmas Eve to scare away the witches. The tradition carried over and became a salute to Christmas. Young men, going from farm to farm, would sneak close to the window and fire shots. Surprisingly, the startled family didn't object. It was considered an honor and in turn the men were invited in for Christmas treats.

Many Scandinavian Christmas customs blend Christian and old pagan traditions—lingering from the time of the ancient sun festival, the time of the winter solstice. During those long, dark, cold nights, it was thought the power of darkness conquered light. Witches were about and evil spirits prowled the countryside. Candles, now a welcome to Christmas visitors, originally protected a family from evil spirits.

Liz Nelson's Norwegian Julekake

"This is my grandmother's recipe which comes via my aunt, Hazel Carlson, Mekinock, North Dakota," says Liz Nelson, Los Gatos, California. "She served it on our last visit. I'd forgotten how delicious it can be when baked by an expert like Aunt Hazel." We eat it with *Geitøst*, a golden Norwegian cheese.

1 cup milk	½-1 tsp. ground cardamom
¼ cup butter	½ tsp. cinnamon
½ cup sugar	3½-4 cups flour
¾ tsp. salt	1 cup golden raisins
1½ pkg. active dry yeast	¼ cup candied red cherries
¼ cup lukewarm water	¼ cup candied mixed fruit
2 tsp. sugar	½ cup blanched, slivered
1 egg, beaten	almonds (optional)
	Lemon Frosting (optional)

Combine milk, butter, sugar, and salt over medium heat until very warm. Add raisins to plump. Set aside to cool. Dissolve yeast and sugar in lukewarm water. Beat egg. Pour off milk mixture from raisins. Add milk and yeast mixtures and spices to egg. Gradually add 2 cups sifted flour and beat 5 minutes with electric mixer.

Pat raisins dry. Combine with chopped candied fruits. Sprinkle with 2 tbsp. flour. Gradually add 1½ cups flour to batter. Turn out onto floured board and knead until smooth and elastic, about 8-10 minutes. Work in fruit and nuts, distributing evenly. Place dough in greased bowl, turning to grease top of dough. Cover and set in warm place until doubled in bulk (about 1½ hours). Punch down and knead lightly.

Form into round loaf, pucker side down, on greased baking sheet or 9-inch greased cake tin. Brush with butter. Cover lightly and set in warm place until almost doubled in size. Bake at 350° for about 1 hour or until bread sounds hollow when tapped. Cool on rack. While hot, brush again with butter and cover with towel to keep top soft. Frost with lemon icing, if desired. Serve with Norwegian *Geitøst.*

Lemon Frosting: Mix 1 cup sifted powdered sugar and 1½ tbsp. lemon juice. The top may be decorated with red and green candied cherries.

Norwegian Lefse

After twenty years of perfecting this old family recipe, here are Liz Nelson's recommendations for her finest *lefse*. Earlier, this thin flat bread, baked on top of the stove, was a simple household staple. Now it is a Christmas delicacy. *Lefse* may be served with butter, sprinkled with sugar, or topped with cheese or preserves. They are best made the day before Christmas.

1½ cups instant mashed potatoes	¼ cup butter
1 cup milk	2½ cups flour
	½ tsp. salt

Prepare mashed potatoes (Liz Nelson uses Betty Crocker Potato Buds) according to directions. (Some *lefse* bakers use fresh baking potatoes peeled, cooked, and riced.) Cool. Scald milk with butter (no margarine). Cool. Combine cooled potatoes, milk, and butter. This will become like a pancake batter. Add sifted flour, a little at a time. Mix well.

With a spoon, dip a piece of dough the size of an egg. On well-floured pastry cloth or board, roll out very thin, into a 10-inch round about one-sixteenth-inch thick. Turn *lefse* frequently to prevent sticking. Roll *lefse* on floured towel and quickly unroll.

Wrap *lefse* around rolling pin and transfer to griddle. Bake *lefse*, one at a time, on ungreased, very hot griddle or skillet (475°) about 2 minutes. When small brown spots appear on underside of *lefse*, turn over, using a long metal spatula. Brown on both sides. Remove from griddle.

If serving immediately, stack and wrap in foil in warm oven. To cool, place between two damp terry cloth towels. Cool to room temperature. *Lefse* should be soft and velvety, not soggy. Wrap in plastic wrap. Place in plastic bag and store in refrigerator. Makes about 12 *lefse*.

Serve warm or at room temperature. Spread with softened butter and sprinkle with brown or white sugar, or top with cheeses or preserves. You may also spread them with sour cream and sugar or with jam

○   ○   ○

In Norway all Christmas preparations must be finished before St. Thomas Day, December 21. Wood must be chopped to last for at least the first three days of the celebration. Cleaning and scrubbing are finished, baking and butchering done. At this time the "peace of Christmas" settles over the land.

Sweden's Lucia Queen

In Sweden Christmas begins on December 13 with the Festival of Lights, or the celebration of St. Lucia Day. Although mainly a home festival, Lucia is honored in schools, offices, and factories of towns and villages throughout the country.

In every family the eldest daughter becomes the Lucia bride, wearing the traditional white robe with red sash, the crown of leaves and candles in her hair. Early in the morning, while it is still dark, she goes from room to room with a tray of saffron buns *(Lussekatter)* and steaming coffee, serving each member of the household in bed.

Italian missionaries, coming to Scandinavia, brought the story of Lucia, the young girl who was blinded and died a Christian martyr. Her day now stands for hospitality and light since the celebration comes near the winter solstice, when nights are long and the sun seldom shines on that day. The coming of the Queen of Light promises that light will return.

Old people of Scandinavia once claimed they could see the Lucia bride between three and four in the morning of December 13, gliding across the icy lakes and snow-covered hills in her white robes, her crown of candles lighting the darkness while she carried food and drink for the parish poor.

The Santa Lucia Song

At Swedish Lucia gatherings, young people, clad in white, entertain with old Advent hymns and Lucia songs. They walk in procession, the Lucia Queen leading the way.

Night goes with silent steps
Round house and cottage.
O'er earth that sun forgot
Dark shadows linger.
Then on our threshold stands
White clad, in candlelight,
Santa Lucia, Santa Lucia.

(English words by Holger Lundbergh)

Swedish Lucia Buns

"When I was a child in Sweden we ate saffron bread all through the Christmas season," chuckles Margit Pettersson Carlson, Santa Clara, California. "Saffron is absolutely essential for Lucia Buns—there are no Lucia Buns without saffron!" she declares.

Treat your family and friends to Margit's delicacy on December 13. Better still, join the Swedes with your own Lucia Queen serving the family breakfast in bed.

1 tsp. saffron threads	2 tsp. sugar
¼ cup boiling water	1 egg
1¾ cups milk	7-7½ cups flour
⅓ cup butter	½ cup blanched slivered
1 cup sugar	almonds
1 tsp. salt	⅔ cup golden raisins
2 pkg. active dry yeast	½ cup candied orange
½ cup lukewarm water	and lemon peel, diced

Soak saffron in boiling water and set aside. (Margit Carlson dries saffron threads in the oven at 200° until crumbly; then mashes them with a sugar cube in a mortar and pestle. She uses additional saffron.)

In a saucepan combine milk and butter over medium heat until very warm. Stir in sugar and salt. Cool to lukewarm. Sprinkle yeast over water and sugar to dissolve. In mixer bowl, beat egg. Add milk/butter and yeast mixtures, saffron, and saffron water. Gradually add 3½-4 cups sifted flour. Beat 5 minutes with electric mixer. Gradually add all but ½ cup flour. Turn dough out onto lightly floured board and knead until smooth and elastic, 8-10 minutes. Gently work in almonds, fruit peel, and raisins, distributing evenly. Place in greased bowl, turning to grease top of dough. Cover with plastic wrap and let rise in warm place until doubled in bulk. Punch dough down.

Lucia Buns: Divide ⅔ of dough into 18 equal pieces, 2½ oz. in weight, or about the size of a lemon. (Set aside remaining ⅓ of dough to make Lucia wreath, if desired.) Roll each piece of dough into a strip, 10 inches long. Form into an S-shape, coiling ends inward (see sketch, p. 272). Place on greased baking sheets. Cover with kitchen towel and let rise in warm place until doubled in size. Brush with 1 egg beaten with 1 tsp. water. Press a dark raisin deep into the center of each coil. Bake at 350° for about 15 minutes. Cool on wire racks, covering buns with terry cloth towel to retain softness. Makes 18 buns. (*Please turn page.*)

Lucia Wreath: With remaining ⅓ of dough, cut dough into equal pieces and roll into ropes. Form wreath according to patterns suggested below. Place wreath on greased baking sheet. Cover and let rise in warm place until doubled in size. Brush with 1 egg beaten with 1 tsp. water. Bake at 350° for 25-30 minutes. Cool on rack.

Lucia Buns are sometimes nicknamed Lucia Cats (*Lussekatter*) or devil's cats—a reminder that evil spirits were thought to be around at the time of the winter solstice when St. Lucia Day was originally celebrated. It is said the devil often took the form of a cat, but his powers could be dispelled by an open display of the same figure—an X with curled tails.

Savor That Saffron

Saffron, the world's most expensive spice, is produced from the stigmas of the purple autumn crocus. Each blossom yields only three stigmas, which must be harvested and packed by hand. 1,000 flowers may yield but one ounce of commercial saffron. Because of its high price, U.S. markets no longer stock it on spice shelves. Customers must ask for it.

"Saffron is now so expensive, many of the Lucia Buns in coffee shops and restaurants are no longer as richly flavored with this spice as before," laments Margaretta Larson, Stockholm. Fortunately, a tiny amount goes a long way.

Swedish Jäst Krans
(Yeast Wreath)

Chewy raisins and nuts fill a wreath of tender, buttery yeast bread. This tasty coffee cake comes from the Swedish kitchen of the late Ruth Peterson of Lindsborg, Kansas.

1 pkg. active dry yeast	4 cups flour
2 tbsp. sugar	1 tsp. salt
1 cup lukewarm milk	1 cup butter or
3 egg yolks	margarine
	Raisin/Nut Filling

Dissolve yeast and sugar in ½ cup lukewarm milk. Set aside. Beat egg yolks until light and lemon-colored. Add remaining ½ cup milk and beat well.

Cut butter into sifted flour and salt and mix as for pie crust. Add yeast, egg, and milk mixtures to flour. Mix thoroughly. Cover and refrigerate overnight. Punch down the next morning. Divide dough in half. On lightly floured board roll one half to 12×18-inch rectangle. Spread with filling. Roll as for jelly roll. Close ends and turn seam side down on greased baking sheet. Shape roll into half moon. Repeat with remaining dough and filling. Cover and set in warm place until doubled in size. Bake at 350° for about 25 minutes or until golden brown. Cool.

Frost with 1 cup powdered sugar and 1½ tbsp. milk.

Raisin/Nut Filling: Beat 3 egg whites until frothy. Gradually add ½ cup sugar and 1 tsp. cinnamon. Beat until stiff. Spread half the egg white on each rectangle. Sprinkle *each* rectangle with ¾ cup raisins and ½ cup chopped walnuts or pecans.

o   o   o

It used to take a lot of bread for the week of Christmas in Sweden. A housewife might bake from sixty to seventy loaves weighing several pounds apiece for a family of six. In most homes they also baked a round loaf called "showbread," made simply of flour and water, but which was beautifully glazed and decorated with dough figures. Not to be eaten, this showbread was treasured and admired until finally crumbled and strewn across the land to ensure a good harvest. (From a record of a Swedish Christmas 100 years ago.)

276

EUROPEAN CHILDREN await the eve of St. Nicholas Day as eagerly as American children anticipate a visit from Santa Claus. On the night of December 6 they polish their shoes with extra care to be set before the fireplace where the good saint may fill them with treats and goodies.

Dressed in a dark homespun robe, St. Nicholas and his helper *Krampus* (he's *Swarte Piet* in Holland) go from house to house. St. Nicholas reads from his little black book of the children's good and bad deeds. Obedient youngsters are rewarded with presents—the others may need a birch switch as reminder. Rumor has it that *Krampus* even stuffs naughty children into his bag and heads for the Black Forest.

Shop windows abound with St. Nicholas treats—delicate chocolates, marzipan pigs, St. Nicholas cookies, and sweets galore to fill little sacks. A German friend, Doris Walter, says her grown children *and,* yes, her husband, still put out their shoes for you-know-who to fill.

Just before St. Nicholas Day in Switzerland, bakeries display rows and rows of little bread men called *Grättimannen* (Basel area) or *Grittibänzen* (Bern area). These funny little fellows who beckon with bright raisin eyes and jaunty caps are eaten for breakfast or supper. The recipe on page 278 comes from the dietitian/cook Erika Nussbaumer, who bakes *Grättimannen* for 50 elderly people in a Basel day care center.

277

Swiss Grättimannen for St. Nicholas Day

These little bread men are sold in bakeries in the German speaking areas of Switzerland for their traditional St. Nicholas Day treat. Large, elaborate *Grättimannen* are often given to children as gifts.

"*Grätti* probably means stickman in Basel dialect," suggests Erika Nussbaumer (who shares the recipe). They are thought to resemble *Schmutzli*, St. Nicholas' helper.

¾ cup milk
⅓ cup butter
⅓ cup sugar
1 tsp. salt
1 pkg. active dry yeast

¼ cup lukewarm water
1 tsp. sugar
1 egg
4-4½ cups flour
Raisins
Egg Glaze

In a saucepan combine milk and butter over medium heat until very warm. Stir in sugar and salt. Cool to lukewarm. Sprinkle yeast over water and sugar. Beat egg in mixer bowl. Add milk/butter and yeast mixtures. Gradually add 2 cups sifted flour and beat 5 minutes with electric mixer. Gradually add 2 cups flour. Turn out onto lightly floured board and knead until smooth and elastic, about 8-10 minutes. Dough should not stick to the board. Place in greased bowl, turning to grease top of dough. Cover with plastic wrap and set in warm place until doubled in bulk. Punch dough down.

Small Grättimannen: Divide dough into 6 equal parts.

1) Roll each piece into a smooth 8-inch oblong body.

2) With the side of your hand, "cut" a head for each *Grätti-annen*, leaving it slightly attached to the body. Place *Grätti-mannen* well apart on large greased baking sheet. Flatten bodies slightly.

3) With a sharp knife or shears, cut arms and legs. Spread legs well apart.

4) Spread arms into different jaunty waving positions.

5) With shears, snip a nose/mouth at the bottom of each face. Cover with kitchen towel and let stand in warm place to rise, about 15 minutes. *(See next page.)*

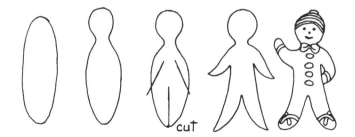

6) Brush each man with 1 egg slightly beaten with 1 tsp. water. Press raisins deep for eyes and buttons. Let rise until doubled in size. Bake at 350° for 15-17 minutes. Watch color closely. Cool on racks. Cover with terry cloth towel to retain soft crust while cooling.

Large Grättimann: Follow mixing instructions. Cut a piece of dough about 1 pound in weight or a little less than ⅔ of the dough. Roll into an oblong body shape about 18-20 inches long. With side of hand, "cut" head and flatten. Place on greased baking sheet. Flatten body of man. Cut legs and arms and spread apart. Continue flattening body and legs.

Form shoes. With small pieces of dough, fashion a stocking cap. Add a little extra flour to remaining dough. Roll out very thin strips of dough (adding a little extra flour) and trim the clothing of the *Grättimann* similar to the decorated clothing in illustration on page 281. With kitchen shears, snip decorative effects into pants and sleeves. Cover with kitchen towel and set in warm place. Let rise until doubled in size. Brush with 1 egg beaten with 1 tsp. water. Sprinkle with *Hagelzucker* or pearl sugar. Bake at 350° for 30 minutes or until golden brown. Cover with foil if necessary to prevent burning. Cool on rack. Cover with terry cloth towel while cooling to preserve softness.

Serve warm, with sweet butter, Gruyere cheese, hot chocolate, tangerines, and peanuts in shell for traditional treat.

281

A Traditional Swiss
St. Nicholas Day Treat

Grättimännli

Gruyere Cheese

Sweet Butter Curls

Marmalades

Orange & Quince

Black Cherry

Hot Chocolate

Mandarin Oranges

Tangerines

Peanuts in Shells

283

Swiss Birnenweggen
(Pear Ring)

Old Swiss cookery features many recipes filled with dried pears, once a staple in rural households. Pears, prunes, raisins, and nuts hide within this moist, ring-shaped loaf.

Dough	*Filling*
¾ cup milk	2 cups dried pears
¼ cup butter	2 tbsp. lemon juice
¼ cup sugar	½ cup brown sugar
½ tsp. salt	½ cup prunes, chopped
1 pkg. active dry yeast	½ cup golden raisins
¼ cup lukewarm water	1 tsp. grated lemon peel
1 tsp. sugar	½ cup walnuts, hazelnuts,
3 egg yolks	or almonds, chopped
1 tsp. grated lemon peel	1 tsp. cinnamon
1 tsp. vanilla	½ tsp. mace
3-3½ cups flour	¼ tsp. nutmeg

In a saucepan combine milk, butter, sugar, and salt until very warm. Cool to lukewarm. Sprinkle yeast and sugar over water. Beat egg yolks until light; add milk/butter and yeast mixtures, lemon peel, vanilla, and mix. Gradually add 2 cups sifted flour and beat 5 minutes with electric mixer. Gradually add remaining flour and turn out onto lightly floured board and knead until smooth and elastic, about 8-10 minutes. Place in greased bowl, turning to grease top of dough. Cover with plastic wrap and set in warm place until doubled in bulk, about 1 hour. Punch dough down.

Knead lightly on floured board. Roll into 20-inch square. Spread with pear filling to within 1 inch of edge. Sprinkle with raisins, prunes, and chopped nuts. Roll up tightly as for jelly roll. Place on greased baking sheet, seam side down. Form into a ring, pinching ends together. With a sharp knife, make crosswise slits about 2 inches apart on top of ring, slashing just to filling or prick steam holes with fork. Cover with kitchen towel and let rise in warm place until doubled in size. Brush with 1 egg beaten with 1 tsp. water. Bake at 350° for about 30-35 minutes or until browned. Cool on sheet 10 minutes. Cool on wire rack. Drizzle with Lemon Frosting, page 265.

Pear Filling: Plump chopped prunes and raisins in hot water. Drain and pat dry. Combine coarsely chopped pears in saucepan with 1 cup water and lemon juice. Simmer, uncovered, until pears are tender and liquid is absorbed. Remove from heat and add brown sugar, cinnamon, mace, and nutmeg (optional: 2 tbsp. *Kirschwasser*). Cool. Spread according to directions and sprinkle with raisins, prunes, and nuts.

"Bread is the head of everything."
—Old Ukrainian folk saying

Among Ukrainian people there is a reverence and honor for bread. More than food, it also becomes part of their religious tradition, used in celebration of life's meaningful occasions.

Ukrainians welcome guests into their homes with an offering of bread and salt. At Christmas, the spectacular three-tiered *Kolach* (symbolizing the Trinity and eternity) centers the family supper table. This same loaf becomes part of a parental blessing when young people marry. *Kolach* is also used in the memorial service for the dead. At Easter, their tall, handsome *Paska* is blessed in church before being eaten at home.

Other occasions, too, merit festive bread. A special loaf at the birth of a new baby. In spring when the birds return, forty birds, fashioned of bread dough, are baked in many households. A farm wife, shaping her bread, cuts the sign of the cross on each loaf. No one gives away the first loaf baked in the oven. Crusts and crumbs are never thrown away.

Indeed, bread accompanies the Ukrainian from birth to death. A gift from God, bread is treated with great respect.

When we sat down to the Christmas Eve meal, my father had prepared a piece of black bread with honey, cut in slices. Starting with my mother and then the oldest child, he went around giving each of us a piece of bread and Christmas greetings, recalls children's author, Marie Halun Bloch, Denver, Colorado.

Ukrainian Kolach

Kolach is a braided ring-shaped bread, used as the traditional table decoration at Christmas. Three braided loaves, topped by a candle, commemorate the Trinity. The ring shape symbolizes eternity. *Kolo* in Ukrainian means circle.

1 pkg. active dry yeast	2 tbsp. sugar
¼ cup lukewarm water	2 tbsp. vegetable oil
1 tsp. sugar	½ cup lukewarm water
3 eggs	4 cups flour
1 tsp. salt	

(For a three-tiered *Kolach*, triple this recipe and repeat directions three times.) Dissolve yeast in warm water with sugar. Beat eggs. Add salt, sugar, oil, lukewarm water; stir in yeast mixture. Add half the sifted flour, 1 cup at a time, and beat 5 minutes with electric mixer. Gradually add remaining flour. Turn onto floured board and knead until smooth and elastic, about 8-10 minutes. Place in greased bowl, turning to grease top of dough. Cover with plastic wrap and set in warm place until doubled in bulk. Punch down. Turn onto lightly floured board.

Directions for Braiding 1 Kolach: (See illustration, p. 290).

1) Divide dough into 6 equal pieces. Roll each piece into a 26-inch strip.

2) Entwine two strips (rope-like fashion), starting at the center. Repeat with remaining strips, making a total of 3 twisted strips.

3) Entwine 2 twisted strips, starting at the center.

4) Join neatly in a circle. Gently brush ends with water to adhere. Overlap slightly. Set in greased low 10-inch round pan. Leave 1-inch space around outer edge.

5) Wrap remaining twisted strip around outer edge of *Kolach* in the 1-inch space around edge of pan. Place a 14-oz. greased can in the center to keep center open. (Can may pop out if *Kolach* pan is too small.)

6) Place in warm spot until almost doubled in size. Brush with 1 beaten egg and 1 tsp. water. Bake at 375° for 10 minutes; reduce heat to 350° for 40 minutes or until *Kolach* is golden in color. Cool.

Repeat 2 more times for three-tiered *Kolach*. Stack 3 loaves and place candle in center.

The *Kolach* is mentioned in some of the oldest Ukrainian Christmas carols. Round or oblong, these braided ropes of dough are a special delicacy from which came the saying, "You cannot entice him, even with a *Kolach*."

"*ON CHRISTMAS EVE* Dad went out to the barn and brought in a bundle of the nicest hay," remembers Sonja Los Shore who grew up in a large Ukrainian community near Winnipeg, Manitoba, Canada. "We children loved to scatter the hay—a reminder of the stable in Bethlehem—around the living room floor. I still remember its fresh, clean, cold smell.

"Mother did a lot of preparation for this day, baking at least a dozen pies, fruit cakes, poppy seed rolls, and a big braided *Kolach* with a Christmas tree in the center. She stored her baking outside—it froze immediately, it was so cold.

"Christmas Eve the whole family went to church. Dad hitched horses to the cutter. He had built a kind of van top for the sleigh with benches and a little stove inside to keep us warm. We drove in the dark, using the light of the moon.

"The day after Christmas—Boxing Day in Canada—carolers came to our house—two groups—one of young, the other of older men. The young fellows always serenaded the oldest teenage daughter (my sister), taking five steps forward and five back. We younger ones thought that very special. Mother had the table set and waiting with a full meal of cabbage rolls, *borscht, pyrizhky*, and Christmas cakes. Wherever they sang, they were offered a meal. A lot of food, yes! But then, they sometimes walked five miles in the snow between farm homes, so they had good appetites."

Have a Merry International Christmas!

First Sunday of Advent

. . . Gather pine boughs to make a wreath with four candles.

. . . Light a candle each Sunday.

. . . Make a family sharing time with carols, Advent readings, poems, and festive treats.

St. Nicholas Day, December 5

. . . Learn about this saintly bishop.

. . . Read "Festival of St. Nicholas" from *Hans Brinker and the Silver Skates.*

. . . Children put shoes by the fireplace and find sweets and trinkets the next morning.

. . . Write limericks and humorous jingles for small-gift exchange.

. . . Serve a Swiss St. Nicholas treat, page 282.

St. Lucia Day, December 13

. . . Celebrate with Swedes. The eldest daughter becomes the Lucia Queen in white gown and leafy crown.

. . . Serve Lucia Buns for breakfast, see page 270.

. . . St. Lucia Day is the Festival of Light. Fill the room with candles.

Christmas Eve and Christmas Day

. . . Take a walk around the Christmas tree, holding hands and singing as they do in Denmark.

. . . Bake an almond in a Christmas rice pudding. The lucky finder gets a marzipan prize—or will get married next year—or will get to do the dishes!!

. . . Scandinavians put out a birds' Christmas tree, a pole with sheaves of wheat tied to the top. Add pieces of bread, suet, and cranberries for extra treats.

. . . Polish families begin their Christmas Eve meal *(Wigilia)* when the first star appears in the evening sky.

. . . Put a little straw under the tablecloth, as Ukrainians do—a reminder of the manger in Bethlehem.

. . . Set an extra plate at the table for an unexpected guest. Polish families believe a guest in the home is God in the home.

. . . Make a German *Bunte Teller*. On this eve each child sets out a plate to be filled with nuts, candies, cookies, fruit. A tiny gift is beside the plate.

. . . Have children write letters to their parents to be read at the Christmas dinner, as Italian children do.

. . . English children love *crackers*. But not the kind you eat! Small favors are hidden inside cylindrical containers. When pulled open, pop! *Crackers* are part of the English Christmas dinner festivity.

New Year's Eve

. . . In Scotland the first person to come into your home in the new year is a *first foot* who brings a piece of coal, bread, a little money, and good fortune. He is honored with food and drink.

Index

294

Thanks to our mothers and grandmothers who kept ancient Christmas customs which have a charm and wisdom all their own.

Traditions are fast fading away. May these remembrances inspire you to preserve the gracious customs of your heritage.